If It's Not Broken . . . Polish It!

What You Need to Know (and Practice) to be a More Successful School Administrator & Organizational Leader (What the Textbooks Don't Tell You!)

O. K. LoVette

UNIVERSITY PRESS OF AMERICA,® INC.
Lanham • Boulder • New York • Toronto • Oxford

Copyright © 2004 by
University Press of America,® Inc.
4501 Forbes Boulevard
Suite 200
Lanham, Maryland 20706
UPA Acquisitions Department (301) 459-3366

PO Box 317
Oxford
OX2 9RU, UK

British Library Cataloging in Publication Information Available

Library of Congress Control Number: 2004108385
ISBN 0-7618-2947-4 (clothbound : alk. ppr.)
ISBN 0-7618-2948-2 (paperback : alk. ppr.)

∞™ The paper used in this publication meets the minimum
requirements of American National Standard for Information
Sciences—Permanence of Paper for Printed Library Materials,
ANSI Z39.48—1992

Contents

Foreword

It is important that you read this brief introduction before you consider the contents of this book. Please read the material with the understanding that these suggestions, tips, admonitions, or whatever you may wish to call them, are not "always" appropriate and do not "always" work. Allow the material to help you as you make decisions, interact with people, and undertake the often overwhelming job of providing leadership in schools and other organizations. It should be noted that much of the material, even though directed toward school settings and school principals, has universal application to leaders and administrators in all types and sizes of organizations. It should also be noted that efforts were made to make the material readable (maybe even enjoyable in places) and "dissertation quality" was not a goal.

It has been one of my goals, during my university teaching career, to help students preparing to be school administrators, to appreciate the value of such terminology as "generally speaking," "In my opinion . . . ," It appears that . . . ," "It has been my experience that . . . ," etc. When you read through the material please accept the items as suggestions and generalizations and not as directives or absolute truths. Even though I feel strongly about the value and utility of the items, their substance will be of naught if not melded with your own personal intellect, reflective experience, and compassion. As there are no proven school or organizational improvement recipes that "fit all," there is no published work that can provide all the answers for all administrative situations. It is my hope that those who will heed and utilize the materials presented will become more effective administrators/managers/leaders while enjoying the benefits of more rewarding personal relationships.

Even though I consider the material contained in this book to be "heavy duty" stuff, much of the material is not supported by "heavy duty" research. Personally, I have a problem with much of the research being conducted. It seems there are so many uncontrollable variables, especially in educational research, that it is difficult or impossible to generalize findings to other situations. As I often remind my graduate classes, some perceive a hierarchy in research that progresses as "lies, damn lies, and statistics." I am sure you have read research that indicated more funding for schools does not result in improved student academic performance. Well, it does in some situations and doesn't in others. It depends on how it is spent, who provides leadership and direction, who it is spent on, and how the statistical analysis was performed.

Most of the information provided is just "good common sense" and the result of over 40 years of experience in the education field, 20 of which were as some type of administrator. It is recognized that what is presented is "just the tip of the iceberg" in terms of what it takes to be an effective leader. Hopefully, university preparation programs have provided strong theoretical and practical bases upon which can be added the knowledge gleaned from individual experiences and the experiences of others (like myself) to help improve performance as leaders in schools and other organizations.

This book has been developed around two basic themes. The first theme primarily relates to relationships with "others;" the second relates to "yourself." Note that we have put "others" before "yourself" which is symbolic (at least from this author's perspective) of the role of school administrators. Of course these two are not distinct categories in terms of interaction, but they seemed appropriate for this presentation. A final section entitled "Final Thoughts" is offered to provide some grit for thought and action.

Preface

ABOUT THE TITLE

Since the early 70's I have kept a poster on my office wall which says: "Man's greatest insanity is to see life as it is rather than as it ought to be." Of course this relates to Don Quixote and Camelot. I have used this as motivation to look for better ways of doing things and have tried to get my students to embrace the idea of "never ending improvement." In so doing, several years ago I came up with the phrase "If it's not broken . . . polish it" and began sharing this maxim with my students. The reason the phrase evolved was because I hated the phrase "If its not broken . . . don't fix it." As far as I was concerned, the later phrase was one of degeneration. I sincerely believed, and still do, if you are not going forward you are going backward. In a similar way, I rejected the statement "That is just the way I am." It is my belief that we all should be making efforts to grow and become better people, to become better at what we do, and in general, to work to improve our lives and the opportunity to impact others.

Acknowledgements

A special thanks to all who have contributed in some way to this "creation." Mr. Darryl Triplett, an inspired and creative art teacher for Monroe City Schools in Monroe, Louisiana created the lively cartoons that helped to make the material lighter and easier to digest. Dr. Joe Savoie, Dean of the Burton College of Education at McNeese State University and Dr. Gene Newman, formerly of the University of Louisiana at Monroe, gave special encouragement and help with editing. Senna LoVette, my wife and Special Education Supervisor, also helped with editing and content based on her present and past experiences as a teacher and school administrator. The biggest "thanks" goes to my students of the past thirteen years who were in my educational leadership courses, and my educator friends of the past forty plus years. I would also like to thank Dr. Marvin Schadt who, as professor and mentor, gave me a new and better perspective on what school leadership should or could be. Finally, I thank God for my health and for the Christian perspective or awareness that helped to shape my convictions, especially about the personal dimension of effective leadership.

Others

This section gives general guidance as to what you "should" and "should not" do as you interact with others. As previously mentioned, what follows are only guidelines and suggestions. However, their regular consideration and use will greatly improve your effectiveness as a leader/administrator/manager.

1. GENERALLY SPEAKING

Never talk down to others (including students)

This may be difficult for some, especially if you are now the boss and perhaps have observed previous bosses who felt like they were entitled, because of their position, to "talk down" to others. Recognize that all people have worth and they want and deserve your respect (at least initially). When you diminish another through your words or deeds you have lost that person as an ally and a supporter and may have created an enemy. There also seems to be a multiplier effect: When that person shares feelings, adverse or otherwise, with friends, relatives, etc., eventually others align themselves with him or her and you have to contend with the social consequences.

Don't paint everyone with the same brush

Just because some are misbehaving, not following directions, etc. does not mean that all are errant. Look for those who are doing what they are supposed to be doing and congratulate and reward them. Try to catch people doing something good. Also, do not be intent on making others into little likenesses of yourself. If you are compulsive and organized that doesn't mean all of those who work with/for you should be the same; heaven forbid. Consider the old saying: "Don't try to teach a pig to sing, it wastes your time and aggravates the pig."

Daryl Triplett
3-D ART©

Don't punish everyone for the sins of a few

It takes courage to call an individual (teacher or subordinate) in to admonish her/him personally about tardiness. It takes only cowardice and stupidity to send a memo to your entire staff admonishing them about tardiness. You will gain the respect of your staff if you will take the hard but productive approach of chastising or reminding *only* those who need it. Even more ridiculous are administrators who make vague comments in a faculty meeting like: "Some of you are not getting to your classes on time. Let me remind you about the possibility for liability when you are late getting to your classroom." A person who does this has not only demonstrated his or her ineptitude, but has also alienated all those who get to school on time, and has publicly displayed his/her personal cowardice.

Give people a good reputation to live up to (sic)

It is hard to hit someone if they have just said something good about you. This simple premise has gotten me through some tough times administratively. One of the most commonly used approaches in conflict resolution is to attempt to remove the emotion and make the discussion more objective. If an angry parent storms into your office and lets fly a few expletives aimed in your direction, your first impulse may be to fire right back at them and perhaps even tell them that "they can't talk to you that way." Well they just did, so what are you going to do about it? Of course, it is generally good technique to allow that person to blow off without interrupting them. It may even require that the police be called. When it is your turn to talk, consider saying something like: "Mr. Jones, I know that you are a concerned parent and only have the best interests of your child in mind. I also know that you are a strong supporter of our school and want to do what will help the teacher to do her best." Now he doesn't want to hit you anymore.

Remember, the use of coercion usually produces a negative reaction (alienation, passive aggression, hatred, etc.). Prisons and the human interaction that happens in them demonstrate this well.

Much of what teachers and students do in the school setting is what they are instructed to do. If people of any age, size, or description are told to do something they don't want to do, guess what? They may do it because there will be some type of negative consequence if they don't, but they may not do it—and the latter to the best of their ability! In fact, they may even try to sabotage directives that seem like they will add to their workloads, or invade their "status quo zone."

A much better approach is to focus on gaining acceptance by allowing all stakeholders, be they teachers or students, to be involved in the development of policies, procedures, etc. If they own the policy by virtue of the fact that they helped formulate it, it will probably be followed, enforced, etc. The kind of power that is to be derived from setting up such collaborative efforts readily organizes a group and is similar to what might be referred to as "peer power." When stakeholders themselves have developed a policy, etc. it becomes theirs, not yours. The informal pressure that this creates is a very powerful aid to securing compliance.

Be nice to your secretary and support staff and openly recognize their value in the operation of the school/business

Support staff can "make or break" an organization. An unpleasant voice answering the telephone, a scowling face behind a receptionist's desk, or a dirty building can have a negative impact on public relations and ultimately organizational effectiveness. Also, the way support staff feel about their jobs influences what they may report in the community. Since they are generally low-paid, they may not feel a strong sense of allegiance to the organization. Administrators must therefore make it one of their major goals, especially in schools, to publicly acknowledge these persons and the important services they provide. Leaders must

make an effort to help them become a part of the "family;" if this happens, then it becomes more difficult to share ugly things about your "family" with the public. One suggestion is to invite these persons to attend staff and other meetings (especially socials), which are otherwise only attended by teachers and administrators. Take every opportunity to provide sincere praise and recognition of your staff in the media and to others within the organization. Verbal recognition in front of peers is also very effective in developing "family" loyalty.

Make your staff/organizational/faculty meetings pleasant and productive

First, make sure all meetings are announced or scheduled well in advance. If possible, have a prepared agenda circulated prior to the meeting. This should help to make the meeting more productive. Do not have meetings to provide information which does not need to be discussed. If you are just "getting the word out," do it with a memo. If you need to make sure everyone gets "the word," ask that a signed copy be returned (C.Y.R., cover your rear). Use meeting time to get in-put from staff members, to develop the "family" identity, and to impart a sense of ownership to those who must implement policies, procedures, etc. Have refreshments of some type for each meeting. Start promptly, but be sure you give yourself ample time for finishing up end-of the day duties.

Don't criticize in public

There are times when you must be critical of a teacher or staff member and also times when you must admonish that person. Be sure all of these sessions are in private and try to hold them only after strong emotions have subsided. If you violate the premise that privacy is of utmost importance, you will destroy your credibility with not only that person but also many of their peers. Also, keep in mind the goals of the organization. If the organization is a school, for example, what are you trying to teach kids about respect for others? School leaders, above all, are expected to model behaviors required of students and staff. Never acquiesce to, or agree with, an upset parent about negative statements they may have made concerning a teacher, even if the teacher has been in the wrong. Once again, correction of the teacher or other employee, if necessary, must always be done in private.

Have a clear understanding of "who does what" and "who's responsible for what;" make sure these details are made known to all staff

Good policies and procedures (P&P) are important for the effective operation of any organization; but just "having them" doesn't necessarily mean
that staff members know what they are. In the ideal situation, staff members would be well-acquainted with the P&P because they helped develop
them, but we know that is generally not the case. When you want people
to become familiar with important materials or information, it is best to
communicate through multiple media—and to do so multiple times. In
other words, use the faculty handbook, repeat your point in memos, discuss in a faculty meeting (for which an agenda was distributed in advance,
highlighting the item you wish to address). It is also helpful to have staff
sign copies of important information and return them to you for your files
(C.Y.R. again). Make sure duty rosters and other types of assignment
sheets are clearly posted, and that they contain a sign-off space in which
individuals can indicate that they are aware of a given responsibility.

Have a forgiving view of people

If you consider yourself a "reflective practitioner" you will be well-
acquainted with the process of reviewing your short-comings and mistakes from the past. Hopefully, you were offered second chances and
benefited from them (note the esteemed position you find yourself in at
present!), and even learned from your miscues. Believing that most people are doing the best they can, or nearly so, will make it possible for
you to be more helpful and generally demonstrate a degree of understanding in your actions toward others. It is important to forgive others
their shortcoming as you would expect to be forgiven, but also to expect
that they will be motivated to improve and overcome their deficiencies
and not continue to make the same mistakes.

Keep McGregor's Theories (X and Y) clearly in mind

If you are not familiar with McGregor's Theory X and Theory Y, let me
give you a brief introduction. In his book, The Human Side of Enter-
prise (1960), McGregor discussed these two theories. Theory X as-
sumed a negative perception of subordinates and Theory Y a positive

perception. He posited that leadership style could influence the behavior of subordinates and subordinate behavior would then support the leader's preferred style. In other words, any effort at group leadership basically became a self-fulfilling prophecy.

I don't teach about many theories or typologies in my classes, but this one I do consider, albeit, in a somewhat modified way. Perhaps perceptions are, in the end, reality. My perceptions cause me to act in certain ways and greatly influence my responses to others and my environment. If an administrator has a positive impression of staff members, he/she will consequently treat them in a positive fashion and they will respond in kind—and conversely. The value of this approach is amplified by previous studies and writings which clearly indicate that people (students and also teachers) often rise to the level of their superiors'/ leaders' expectations. This is especially true if they are reinforced with positive feedback and positive assessments and, if the superiors are recognized as genuinely believing in the abilities of others.

2. SELECTING TEACHERS

Spend time finding teachers and employees who "care," then "care" for them

No administrative task is more important than selecting the right person for a given position. Locate the right people, place them in the job, and let them do their work! Once you have the right people in the right positions your job should be easier. You need only make sure they have what they need to do the job, and they feel rewarded for doing it. It is your responsibility to facilitate and maximize their performance. Having good teachers (and employees) doing their jobs well (and enjoying their work) can demonstrate how effective you are as a leader!

Seek out teachers who sincerely care about students, have a good sense of humor, are not afraid to change, and are willing to spend the time it takes to improve student learning

If you can find this kind of teacher, then, by all means, go after him or her! The difficulty lies in trying to determine if a prospect has these qualities. The best indication of an applicant's classroom potential will generally come from a previous employer, that is, when references can be obtained. If they cannot, it is a good idea to develop a set of interview questions which can enable you to check for these desirable qualities. Getting help from some of the teachers already on your faculty is also a good idea. Ask them to assist you in developing scenarios or questions which will allow you to identify desirable qualities, and then join you in the interview.

Parents who have raised kids often make good teachers

It has been my experience that a mature person, often a mother who has raised a family (at least gotten them all in school), is often likely to become a very productive teacher. These persons are usually very stable, willing to learn, and anxious to do a good job.

Use various scenarios when interviewing and, wherever possible, involve faculty in the selection of new teachers

The scenario approach can provide better information about a prospective teacher than questions which might allow them to use "canned" answers. As noted above, involving faculty members in the development of these scenarios and allowing them to participate in an interview can be very helpful. Those who participate in the hiring effort will justifiably feel a sense of the importance of their input, partial ownership of the process, and, consequently, a sense of responsibility toward a person who is selected. They will want that person to succeed because they helped select them. New teachers who are selected by some other process often have two strikes against them when they join the staff. They are not always received warmly by those already on faculty, especially if they are young, enthusiastic, and full of new ideas.

3. WORKING WITH TEACHERS

Spend most of your evaluation/supervision time with those who need it most

Your evaluation policies and procedures may require that you be equally diligent with all teachers or employees. Even if this is the case, it is still advisable to "fudge" a bit and spend more time with those who seem to need it most. Some of your staff members need only your support, encouragement, supplies, equipment, etc. to facilitate their teaching or other activities. Others may need a lot of attention, and even correction.

We could salvage a lot of new teachers, and even some mature ones, if we could give them the time and assistance they need.

Support your teachers in the presence of others

Even though you may have to correct a teacher in private, you should not fail to support him or her until you have all the facts about some troublesome circumstance that may have arisen. One of the best ways to destroy faculty morale is to correct or admonish a teacher in front of a student, parent, or other teacher. News of this sort of thing travels fast.

Remember, if it's not my idea, I may not support it.

Whether or not a teacher or employee will support your ideas will probably depend on how that person feels about you—and about the person who came up with the idea in the first place. When people are confronted with the possibility of some change which may add to their workload, their natural response is: "What's in it for me?" "How much time and energy will I have to expend?" Don't forget this! Think about what you would say if they actually had the audacity to ask straight out: "What's in it for me?"

Let the teachers count the votes

Of course they trust you! Don't kid yourself. Put yourself, other administrators, and others within your direct sphere of influence (secretaries, bookkeepers, counselors, etc.) beyond suspicion. It should never occur to them that you might be trying to make things "come out your way," or somehow attempting to benefit from their work. Let the teachers count votes, for example, when you are voting on calendars, teacher of the year, etc. Also, when administering some type of survey or questionnaire, be sure that teachers are guaranteed anonymity—only this can ensure valid responses. Have them collected by someone other than yourself or your immediate staff, and make sure that it does not look in any way like the responder can be identified. Teachers are generally a very suspicious bunch—often for good reasons.

All evaluation and supervision must be "formative"

The two basic types of evaluation often discussed in courses relative to supervision are "summative" and "formative." Summative evaluation is generally the norm. It includes one supervisory visit (often abbreviated) near the end of the school year as some type of "final" evaluation. Unfortunately, such evaluations have proven to be essentially useless when it comes to improving instruction or any other aspect of classroom performance. If we are really trying to use valuable administrative time productively to improve instruction, production, etc. we should use a formative approach. Such a process is initiated near the beginning of the school year, includes several conferences, and concludes near the end of the year with planning for next year's growth and improvement. Included in it are discussions about plans and strategies for effective instruction, and several classroom observations. Administrators often complain that they don't have time to give to this lengthier process, but, by objecting in this way, they are negating the importance of close contact with their teachers and hands-on assessment of their classroom performance.

Learn to say "no" in a firm, tactful, reasoned, and polite way

Most of us don't like to say "no," especially to friends or peers. But, even though politeness and reason should always temper the effective

leader's interaction with his/her staff, there are definitely times when you must say "no." Doing so shouldn't come easy. It should come after an unemotional evaluation of the facts and be accompanied by some reasoned explanation. (No you cannot take your class on a field trip to the mall! It was not planned as reinforcement for part of your curriculum. The request was not submitted in a timely fashion. The superintendent has said there will be no more trips this year. The funds are not available. Last time we had vendors who reported that our students had been loud and rowdy, and it was reported that some may have stolen small items.) Of course, you won't need to supply this many reasons, but the person putting demands on you will feel more like you are trying to be fair if you have a reason(s).

People are basically hedonistic (and teachers are people)

Maybe "hedonistic" is too strong a word, but we all (or most) have comfort zones and also routines that we try to maintain. In fact, most of us would like to find things that would make life easier, not more difficult, than it is. We would like to find a little more pleasure in what we do. This fact often makes change and improvement difficult. Most of us are not seeking more demanding work or a change in our comfortable (or tolerable) situations, but rather more pleasurable, less stressful work.

Spend a lot of time with new teachers

The mortality rate among new teachers is very high, and, most often, they say their reason for leaving the profession is not the pay. Why do new teachers (especially those during their first 5 years) abandon their dream of becoming a teacher? Often it is because administrators haven't taken the time to help them have a good first year. New teachers need a good orientation program and help in becoming a part of the school "family." Administrators should also be pro-active in anticipating their problems. This can be done on the basis of past experience (and existing research), and programs which anticipate their needs and assist them as appropriate. How many new teachers have just been handed a set of keys and told their room was just down the hall? And, maybe it would also be good to avoid giving the new teachers all the toughest students and the most difficult class assignments.

Develop a good orientation program

As mentioned, a good orientation program should be in place at the start of the year, and it should constantly be refined. The process should start immediately after, if not before, a new teacher is hired. What can be done to welcome that person to the community and the school? Do they need help finding a place to live? Do they need an advance on their salary, a paycheck after the first week or so, or perhaps a short-term loan? What about a tour of the community, school, and central office? Giving them a chance to meet other staff members and new teachers in an informal, get-acquainted setting might be nice. Of course, new employees will also need to know about the rules and regulations, be assigned a mentor or buddy teacher (one that cares!), and be supported throughout the year. Whatever the components of your orientation program may be, it should be developed with extensive involvement of young staff members, evaluated near the end of each year, and, subsequently, refined. (It may not be broken, but we can certainly polish it!)

Give special care to your substitutes

The job I would want least would be that of substitute teacher, especially in a difficult setting at the secondary level. It goes without saying that substituting is a thankless job and often with very low pay. What substitutes do is often considered "babysitting" and, most of the time they are in charge, not much learning happens. If we believe that "time on task" is critical to student learning, administrators must consider what can be done to help these persons be more productive and make the experience more pleasurable and rewarding. A more appropriate wage would help to attract more capable teachers, but this may not be feasible in many situations, so we must also look for other approaches to enhance the desirability of this work.

Those who do substitute teaching need to know they are an important part of the school's operation. Special training (paid) should be provided for them (especially in classroom management) and they should be invited to staff activities (workshops, faculty meetings, socials, etc.). What about a pass to athletic events? If substitutes feel like they are a part of the school "family," they will feel more of a sense of responsibility for student learning and also more loyalty to the school. Substitutes who have bad experiences in your school are often bearers of the "bad tidings" to the community. Also, teachers may have to adopt a more supportive attitude and make sure they are adequately prepared for those occasions when a substitute must be called upon. Of course, it probably goes without saying, you should evaluate your program yearly and continue to work out any glitches it may have.

4. MOTIVATING

Give others "a good reputation to live up to"

The thought that "It's hard to hit someone if they have just said something good about you" (noted earlier), is definitely worth keeping in mind, especially in conflict situations: "Mr. Jones, I know you are very angry right now, and I also know how concerned you are about the welfare of children. You are one of our best supporters of the athletic program and also our academic programs. I know you have spent hours flipping burgers so the booster club could buy new uniforms for the team." After he has heard this coming from you, Mr. Jones will have a hard time with his earlier desire to hit you. This is one of the most effective ways I have found for getting others to aspire to, and achieve at, higher levels of performance. Sincere praise and recognition for achievements and efforts have a magical effect on many of us, especially when it is delivered in front of peers and the community.

Catch people "doing things right"

An important part of an administrator's or supervisor's job is being "visible," as opposed to hiding in one's office and not being available to people. Being out in the halls and in classrooms is very important— "when the cat is away the mice will play." This may be something of an overstatement, but most of us would probably agree that we tend to perform at higher levels when we are aware that someone might be watching. However, it should not be your goal as an administrator to "catch people doing something wrong or bad;" rather, your purpose should be to reinforce good and appropriate behavior by "catching people doing things right," especially by invitation. When you learn that some special class activity is going to take place, ask for an invitation. Better yet, ask your teachers to invite you whenever they have something they would like you or others to see. It is then up to you to attend whenever possible and extend the compliments and praise to students, teachers, etc.

Have a suggestion box to be used by anyone

People need a way to express their dissatisfaction (and, also, their satisfaction) privately. A suggestion box makes a statement about your administration's willingness to listen to others' concerns and to consider implementing changes as they seem necessary. You must, however, be certain to be responsive to suggestions (at least some of the time) so that contributors know it is not something you are using, as a sort of prop, just to appease any need they might have to complain.

Learn all your staff members' names (right away) and use them often

Spend whatever time is necessary to learn your teachers' and other staff members' names immediately after they are hired. This must be a priority. A bulletin board containing all the teachers' and other staff members' pictures, with names attached, is also highly desirable. It should be displayed prominently in the reception area of your school or in the entryway. You should also make similar efforts to learn student and parent names. People like to hear their names, consequently, learning names is not enough; you must also use them on a regular basis. I prefer to refer to staff members using their titles of respect. e.g. Mrs. Smith or Dr. Twiddle, since it seems to me that many schools have become much too informal. Using these titles and insisting that students and teachers do likewise can help maintain (or restore, as the case may be) an atmosphere of respect for school employees, other students, and the institution in general.

Accentuate and build on the positive features of your school

All schools have positive aspects, and these can become the foundation upon which improvements can be made. Sometimes, it may seem there are so many negatives in a school setting that it is impossible to recognize any positives. This means that we need a reassessment and a "blessing counting" session—a faculty/staff meeting, where the agenda (announced in advance) will include enumerating the many strengths and positive aspects of the school. This can help staff overlook any causes of stress and focus on the positives. The next step in such a meeting is to begin discussing how to build on these known strengths (these meetings should continue on a regular basis as well). This may seem pretty idealistic, or even simplistic, but it has the potential to improve the social climate at your school and it is a tool often overlooked. The process of asking people to focus and build on the institutional strengths can be very powerful indeed, and can lead to significant efforts to improve.

Low teacher morale is contagious

Recognize that it is your job as an official leader to help teachers and other staff members maintain positive feelings about their work situations. The often heard saying: "A bad apple will spoil the whole barrel," can also apply to staff morale. Fortunately, we are not apples in a barrel, but where we all find ourselves gathered for the spoiling process is generally the faculty "lounge." Your responsibility as an administrator must be to make the "workroom" (my preferred terminology) a pleasant, productive place which helps to boost teacher morale. Surprise treats, notes of congratulation, quiet music (perhaps), comfortable furniture, etc. can be used to make this area special. It also is important that you enlist the help of key staff members (some just seem to always have a positive attitude) to help with planning such activities.

Give others the credit! It will come back to you
many times over

Get used to not saying "I" all of the time. If you really want to see others blossom, you must practice giving them credit. You must say "our team (or even "our teachers") did a great job of preparing the new curriculum" even though you were the leader and did much of the work. This type of approach has many potential benefits. Those who were given the praise will see you as not being selfish, will be inclined to be more productive, and will have more respect for your leadership!

Never miss an opportunity to compliment or say something encouraging to someone

Whether in the school setting or in public, don't miss chances to compliment and encourage the individual efforts and accomplishments of others. Students appreciate your acknowledgement of their successes when you personally compliment them for their athletic achievements, success in a theatrical event, outstanding test scores, etc. Teachers appreciate your compliments and encouragement just as much, perhaps more, than students. Your actions also serve as a model for students and teachers and may also impact their desire to compliment and encourage others.

Honor and recognize students and others as often and sincerely as possible

Honor and recognition must be freely given, but sincerely. Public announcements and recognition are inspiring to most of us and cause us to aspire to greater levels of accomplishment and effort, so don't miss an opportunity to publicly recognize the successes of others whether in an assembly, on the intercom, or in the media. Honor and recognition given to employees, students, and even parents can have a positive effect on the climate of a school and is contagious for most of us. There are always a few who are not affected, or are even negatively impacted by praise and compliments. Try to avoid these persons—don't waste your time with them.

5. EMPOWERING

Don't feel like you have to do it all yourself

Two heads are better than one and surely 30 heads are better than 1, at least the potential is much greater. You may be good but you are not that good! Why not tap the potential of others and save yourself time and effort by utilizing their talents, abilities, brain power, and energies? Even if you are the type of person who feels they must "be on top of everything," hopefully, you are intelligent enough to see the disadvantages of trying to maintain that position. This should be especially evident to school leaders who are faced with new responsibilities almost on a daily basis.

Many of your staff members are probably just as capable and intelligent as you are

Need I say more? You were just the one that got the job. You say your uncle was on the school board?

Share ownership with stakeholders

At this point, this statement should be redundant. The benefits to be derived from sharing ownership are well-grounded in the research and highlighted in this work. This doesn't mean you have to share ownership with those who are not stakeholders, but you might still ask for their input. People like to feel they have some control over factors that impact their use of their time, their workloads, and especially their pocket books (directly or indirectly). Shared ownership generally means shared responsibility and most leaders would certainly prefer that others shared the myriad of responsibilities associated with educating today's children.

Decision making: When to share it and when not to, and how to set parameters for doing so

Leaders with administrative responsibilities are paid "big bucks" (This is a joke, too!) to make decisions. Many of these decisions do not require the input of staff members, let alone the need to share the decision making process. However, if and when we do choose to involve others in this process, we must be sure to carefully establish the parameters, and be clear in advance on how the resulting decision will be accepted and/or applied. For example, if you empower a school committee to develop a discipline policy, you must first clearly communicate (best done in writing) any of the limits which have been placed on the committee or its decision (e.g. A new policy may not involve any new costs to the school or district, may not conflict with any existing board policies, and may not impose any additional requirements on the school administrator's time). You must be able to accept and support the policy developed by the committee, otherwise you must communicate to them that it will only be used as input. Fortunately, or unfortunately, faculty may be pleased merely to have input, a clear indication that some administrators fail to recognize its value.

Many hands make heavy work light

Besides making your job easier, when you allow staff members to help you in some way with your responsibilities, you are allowing others the opportunity to feel a sense of importance, involvement, and hopefully, some recognition. You must also be aware that involving the "wrong hands" at the "wrong time" may be counterproductive. Opening the doors to involvement in the decision making process just for the sake of saying you are involving others, can also make a wrong impression lead to a lack of trust in the leadership.

6. COMMUNICATING

Don't have a faculty meeting just to give information

Don't hold a faculty meeting if all you intend to do is provide information. Faculty meetings should be called when you need to get faculty input or to discuss a topic or situation with them; meaning that they will also be talking! When feasible, information should be provided via memo, e-mail, or other methods that do not require everyone's attendance at the same time and in the same place. If you fear that some of your faculty will toss memos without reading them, ask that each keep a loose leaf binder to keep the year's memos, etc. To make sure the material has been read (as sure as you can be), you might also ask that, after reading, they sign it and drop it off in the office, after making a copy for their binder. It is also important that the administrator have faculty meetings at a predetermined time and on days that have been reserved for them. A memo regarding a meeting might state: "Please reserve the following dates and times for our faculty meetings this year: the first and third Tuesday of each month from 3:15 until 4:15. Our meetings will be held in the cafeteria unless otherwise announced. An agenda will be available at least two days prior to each meeting (when feasible) and minutes from each meeting will be posted in the 'workroom.' To have an item placed on the agenda, please contact the principal/administrator in advance of the meeting."

Your staff will appreciate it if you provide some type of refreshment for each faculty meeting; another tactic is to ask parents to provide something. Also, remember to invite those who substitute for you as well as available support staff, so they can also feel that they are part of the family.

Be sure to tap into the grapevine

What passes through the grapevine is not always completely factual, but it has a major impact on what people are thinking and doing. Recognizing that many of the informal activities within an organization may have more influence on peoples' actions than do formal directives is imperative for organizational leaders. The more information you have, the better your decisions can be. Also, who likes to be "blind-sided?" Identify in advance, wherever possible, those members of your staff who can provide information (hopefully also accurate information) that will be useful to you in performing your duties.

It is also a good idea to identify the "key communicators" in your community and cultivate their friendships. Often, they can indeed provide helpful information, especially about the community's perceptions about what is "going on up there." "Key communicators" come in a variety of shapes and sizes; they may be your local barber/beautician, ministers, a used car sales person, a banker, etc.

KISS (Keep it simple, stupid)

The terminology we use with each other may have little meaning to our patrons. Any and all efforts you make to avoid sending out lengthy, convoluted messages to the public will be appreciated; your staff will also be grateful for directness, clarity, and brevity in your communications.

When you can communicate something without having a meeting, do it

Meetings (with an agenda) should only be scheduled when you need to engage in two-way communication. If you are merely providing information, do it with a memo. Each meeting should also be followed with some type of minutes which record actions, directives, etc. Be sure all meetings take place at the time they were initially scheduled.

Be a good and active listener

Practice using body language that says I hear you (I may not agree, but I hear you.) Provide affirmations when possible, and avoid making the other person feel they are less important or have less status than you. If you cannot give your full attention to someone at a meeting, you might ask the person to send you a memo or e-mail you so you can give their question more thought. It is perfectly acceptable (and, in fact, a respectful gesture) to tell that person your attention is divided right now and you would be able to focus on their question better at another time.

Saying it once won't get the job done

If your message is very important and something that everyone must receive and understand, use multiple media and send out multiple messages. This means you get your message out there several times using various types of media (bulletins, announcements, news release, etc.) It may seem that you should not have to repeat yourself, but the fact is that we are all bombarded with useless information much of the time, and just because it came from the boss does not, of necessity, make it a priority item.

All talk about students should be positive

Your talk and your teachers' talk about students should always be constructive (Take the high ground!). In our litigious society, this is also the safest approach.

Make sure the rules and regulations are clear and understood by everyone

Everyone likes to know where they stand, what they can and can't do, what the rules are, and also how the rules will be enforced. (In the case of the latter, hopefully it will be consistently.) If you make all the necessary efforts to insure that everyone understands the rules and regulations, you will avoid many problems. To ensure maximum adherence to rules and regulations, teachers and/or students should be allowed participation in their development. When appropriate, allow those who will be charged with enforcing them or governed by them to make the rules and regulations (within parameters that may be established by policy, law, or your direction).

Refuse to talk negatively about others

Don't gossip, don't listen to gossip, and admonish others when they are gossiping. Accentuate the positive and require others to practice finding good in situations and people. Start meetings with some time for sharing the "good" things that have happened recently. Make sure all "testimony" is brief and upbeat.

Never assume your message was received as you intended it

As previously noted, it is a good idea to have a friendly staff member who can "tip you off" when your message has not been received as intended. Some might consider this person a "spy" or "informant," but it is important (not only for your sake, but for the same of the school and community as a whole) to have advance warning when something you have said has been misconstrued.

The physical appearance of your school communicates a great deal to visitors and those who pass-by

It may not be fair, but patrons or others who visit your school or just pass-by are either positively or negatively influenced by how your school looks. Is the outside well-kept? Has the grass been mowed and trimmed? Is the paint peeling? Does it look like a place where children should be? What about the inside? Does it feel and look like a warm, hospitable place? Is it clean and in good repair? If this is something which does not seem very important to you and consequently does not get a lot of your attention or time, I would suggest having a building committee give their time and consideration to such matters. Make sure the people on this committee value cleanliness and orderliness of appearance. Ideally, such a committee could be constituted of two or three teachers, a custodian, a cook, and at least one parent.

"I don't know" and "I'm sorry" are valid parts of your vocabulary and should probably be used more often

Do you "know it all?" Of course you don't—and you may know less than many of those who are working for you! You were probably not placed in your administrative position because of your knowledge and command of information, but because of your leadership abilities. Knowledge and information can certainly help you be a more effective leader, but effectively tapping into and properly utilizing the abilities and knowledge of others can make you a great one. Simply acknowledging that you don't have all the answers can have an empowering effect on those who depend on you for leadership. They will probably appreciate the fact that you aren't arrogant enough to pretend that you do: "Maybe he/she is human after all!"

Some of us also have a hard time admitting we are/were wrong, more so it seems, when we become administrators. (Maybe our newly inflated egos tend to get in the way!) To err is human, so if we don't err we must be inhuman. Mistakes are best corrected rather than covered up. Be honest and forthright in correcting your mistakes (just try to keep the number of them low) and you will be more respected by those you lead.

7. FACILITATING

Take care of the little things

I subscribe to what I would call a modified Hygiene Theory[1] which partially relates to "satisfiers" and "dissatisfiers" in the work environment. It is my belief that the concepts within the Hygiene Theory are valid and should be well-understood by school and other leaders. It is easy to acknowledge, and well-supported by research, that there are certain factors such as respect, recognition, and praise, "satisfiers," which can make us feel good about ourselves and our jobs. It is also very important to recognize that there may be small annoyances or "dissatisfiers" within the work environment which may diminish the effect of the "satisfiers." If you recognize the importance of this concept/theory, you will also understand the importance of making sure pencil sharpeners work, lights are not blinking, and classes are not always being interrupted by the intercom. (The importance of taking care of the little things will be discussed in more detail in the context of discussion of the LoVette Leadership Model.)

Remember Maslow?

It is imperative that leaders be familiar with Maslow's Hierarchy of Needs as Motivators[2]. Maslow identified several levels of needs which act as "motivators" until they are met. The lowest level relates to basic physiological needs such as food, air, water, sleep, etc.; the next level relates to safety; the third to social needs, or the need to belong; and the higher order "motivators" relate to esteem and self-actualization. The concept is simple and easy to apply, especially at the lowest level of the Hierarchy. Consider the violence which is becoming more prevalent in many of our schools; if students/teachers are concerned about their own personal safety, their primary motivations may be to keep themselves safe. Consequently, motivation to belong, etc. (higher order motivators) may cease to be operative.

Leaders must be aware of those motivations which may be hindering, as well as promoting, employee and even student performance. In other words, a school administrator must take care of those things that might be keeping students from learning and teachers from teaching. A good example would relate to food service programs. If students are hungry when they come to school, they will not be effective learners because their motivation is to get something to eat and that is where their thoughts will be. Consequently, we feed them so that they are not motivated by hunger and can aspire toward higher levels of development. This application probably wouldn't be totally acceptable to Maslow, but I would argue that it is valid.

A major part of your job is to serve your teachers

If you can think of yourself as a facilitator for your staff, rather than the "boss," you are probably well on your way to becoming a more effective leader. The LoVette Leadership Model (LLM) mentioned earlier was designed for use in leadership classes, but it can be applied in any organizational setting. The Model is sketchy in its design because it was intended to introduce for discussion three major traits of leaders of today and tomorrow. The bottom part of the pyramid is large and basic. At this level, "Facilitation," is the major role of the leader—something which might also seem closely akin to the "dissatifiers" discussed earlier. The leader must see that the little things (as seen by some) are taken care of so teachers and others can do their jobs effectively. A part of the responsibilities of a leader is merely doing the organization his service of facilitating everyone's work—making sure the building is clean, supplies are available, the duty schedule is posted, and so on.

The next level (the smaller segment of the pyramid) relates to "Empowerment." This concept, which is somewhat modern and still foreign to many administrators, involves sharing power and ownership (of decisions, etc.) as well as responsibility, e.g. If a faculty has developed a school discipline policy, they own the policy and consequently will work to see that it is applied. Even giving the staff input on such a matter as this (again, making sure it is understood that it is only "input") can have a positive impact on the attitude and actions of your staff. Often, teachers complain that they are left out of decision-making. Their complaints may indeed be justified since they are the major stakeholders in the institution, its processes and goals, and, also, often the persons most often held accountable for results.

The narrow, top portion of the pyramid relates to "Vision"—something notoriously difficult to describe. Present day literature often discusses the "visionary leader" and his or her work toward realizing a personal vision(s). I take exception to part of that, namely that leaders should always have visions of what should or could be. The fact is that most of those visions cannot be accomplished without the efforts of others, e.g. If the leader has a vision of a school where discipline is not a major issue, that leader may have empowered (second level of the pyramid) the teachers to develop a discipline policy. When that policy has been developed and implemented, teachers will have ownership of institutional processes, and strong normative pressure (roughly equivalent to peer pressure) will be in place to help maintain faculty support and ensure adherence to rules. A major role for the leader then becomes that of keeping the vision present to the minds of the faculty through monitoring, supervising, and facilitating.

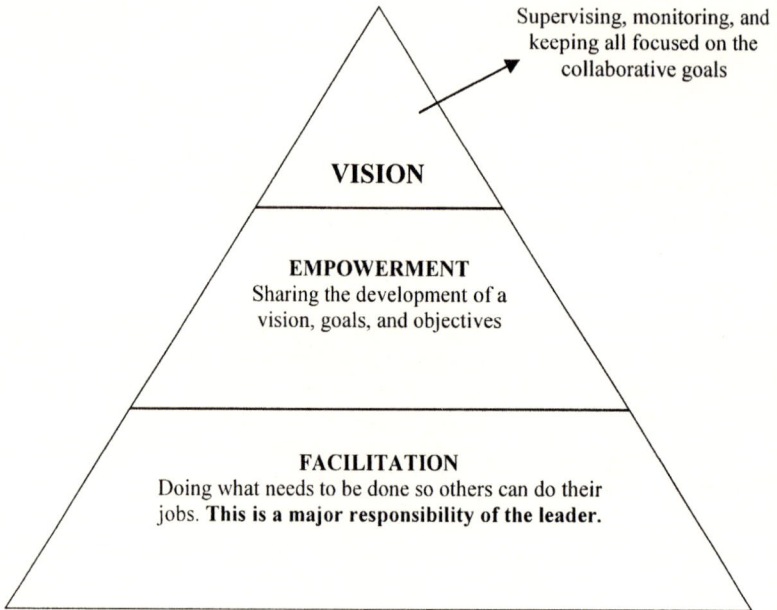

Supervising, monitoring, and keeping all focused on the collaborative goals

VISION

EMPOWERMENT
Sharing the development of a vision, goals, and objectives

FACILITATION
Doing what needs to be done so others can do their jobs. **This is a major responsibility of the leader.**

Work to reduce risks in the school environment by reducing uncertainty

The modern concept of a contingency approach would dictate that we do more than be pro-active. It would imply that we work to anticipate what might happen, especially negative events, in the work/study environment and have a plan for a response—if "this" happens then we will do "this." For example, if there is a tornado warning, we will sound three brief bells followed by three more and teachers will have students move to the inner halls of the building. If we have a dangerous situation with someone who might have a firearm we will say "code red" over the intercom and all teachers will lock their doors and keep students inside. When the copier is not working, we will take all items to be copied to the central office at 10:00 each morning and will return copied items to teachers, students and/or staff by noon.

8. IMPROVING STAFF

Spend money on staff development

Business and industry often spends as much as 5% of their budgets on developmental activities for their staffs. It is rare for schools or even districts to spend even 1% on such activities. Just allocating more resources will not necessarily result in more effective professional development, but, conversely, it is certainly difficult to schedule needed activities if the funds are not available.

Staff development should not be a "one shot deal"

Much of what passes for staff development is a "one shot" presentation that is soon forgotten. Maybe the expensive presentation was inspirational and entertaining, but generally, we don't even remember the jokes after a few days. For staff development to be effective it should be continuous and related to staff needs and interests. Old habits are hard to break. When we have been taught a certain way (K–12), we tend to teach much the same way, even though we may receive vastly different training in our college programs. This should cause us to realize that teachers will not greatly change what they are doing after attending a "one-shot" staff development session.

My concept of staff development is much larger than that generally discussed in the professional literature. My definition of staff development (the phrase "professional development" is preferable) would include any activity designed to improve a teacher's overall performance. Activities that might qualify would include travel for a geography teacher, a college course on adolescent psychology, or even a bird census for a biology teacher.

Train selected teachers
to be your staff development professionals

To save a few dollars and generate a cadre of local professionals, many districts are training their own teachers or staff members to take the role of staff development specialists. The expense may seem great, but the benefits are many. You will then have trained development professionals in-house who can provide appropriate activities whenever needed. Moreover, good public relations with staff and community can result from such expenditures.

Identify and train those who would be effective mentors for new teachers/staff members

New teachers and other staff members need all the help they can get. A ready source for this help is the existing staff. Which of your staff members has the personality and energy necessary for helping new people? Once you have identified these helpers, they will need training on how they should approach their task; abundant recognition and praise for their efforts is also a good idea, particularly where you can't provide the appropriate additional compensation. It is a fact that many new teachers leave the profession after a short period of time—a trend which has become a major problem in our schools. A trained, caring mentor can help us retain much-needed new staff members and also assist them in being more effective.

9. DISCIPLINING

When you must chastise a teacher or student, do it in private

Nothing says more about your ineptness than chastising a teacher or a student in front of others, especially peers. Perhaps you can recall when you were a student and a teacher may have "chewed out" a student for some classroom violation. No doubt, you felt sorry for the student and anger toward the teacher, even though the student was in the wrong. Think about it! Make sure you always chastise privately, but it is highly desirable to praise in-public.

Always tell a teacher what you did to discipline a child

Often, teachers are critical of the discipline imposed on a student by their principal. But, maybe the principal didn't convey the relevant information effectively to the teacher or teachers. To remedy this, I suggest the use of a referral form to be returned to the teacher or teachers. It should advise on the disciplinary action taken and provide any other information or direction necessary. This technique alone can solve a lot of problems and improve communication.

Don't allow teachers to send all their problems to you

First of all, don't let your desk be the dumping ground for problems which should be handled in the classroom. Too often principals allow themselves to be bombarded with minor discipline problems that are clearly the responsibility of the teacher. e.g. "Johnny was leaning back in his chair." "Joe broke Tony's pencil." "Joanne was caught cheating." Discipline is part of the teaching job; you are there to back up the teachers, and to handle major discipline issues when they arise.

"Don't bring me a problem without possible solutions." Let your staff know that they can't just dump all their problems on you and leave. Make it clear to them that you expect them to have thought through the problems (at least most of the time) and to come to your office ready to offer some possible solutions. This approach can be extremely helpful to you as an administrator. It also requires teachers to use their general knowledge of human nature and their problem-solving abilities (something which often makes them feel good).

Daryl Triplett
3·D ART

A few admonitions for those who choose to use corporal punishment

Corporal punishment has been banned in a large number of states, but where it is still practiced, it should be administered according to pre-scribed policies and should clearly serve as a deterrent to future mis-behavior. Consider this: "Never paddle a student twice in the same day for the same type of offense." If it didn't work the first time, what makes you think it will work the second time? You need to look in your "bag of tricks" to see if some other form of discipline might pro-duce the desired results. Some of the reasons corporal punishment has been disallowed in so many states include the fact that those ad-ministering it may have been overly zealous, some did not follow prescribed procedures, or such procedures were not available; an-other reason is simply the fact that our society has become increas-ingly litigious. We have become "lawsuit happy"—it seems there is always an attorney who will file a suit and represent the injured party free of charge, so as to get a large percentage of any award when the case is finally resolved.

Be sure to consider the following when administering corporal punishment:

1. Have relevant policies and procedures in place and make sure they have been approved by your board of education.
2. Follow these policies and procedures religiously and document your actions.
3. Never paddle a student twice during the same day for the same type of offense.
4. The "paddler" should not be angry when applying the punishment. This generally means someone other than a teacher should be doing it.
5. Always have a witness when administering corporal punishment.
6. Many parents don't want anyone (including themselves) to physi-cally punish their child.
7. If you administer corporal punishment, be sure you have liability in-surance and a good attorney.

10. WORKING WITH STUDENTS

Respect students

If we expect to have the respect of students, we must first respect them. Teachers who can be identified as lacking in respect for students either need a major attitude adjustment, or they need to find a new line of work. "Do unto others as you would have them do unto you" is quite appropriate in such cases.

Education is a "right" not a "privilege"

Remember when we used to tell our students how fortunate they were to have the privilege of attending school—and also that privilege could be removed if they didn't act properly? Well, times have changed; the courts have seen to that. Students do not shed their rights just because they have entered the school doors. They now enjoy the "right" to attend our schools, and for us to remove that right involves extensive due process. Along with this right comes a number of others rights that must be protected by those charged with educating in a safe, nurturing, democratic environment.

Be careful about kicking kids off a team without giving them a semblance of due process

A student's "right" to participate in extracurricular activities is a somewhat cloudy issue, and certainly fertile ground for litigation. It is very important that student participants know the expectations of the coach, the school, and any relevant governing associations. This information should be provided to them in the form of a document. It should include a statement of the penalties to be incurred for not adhering, and should be signed by both the parents and the student. Student expulsion from a team or organization should be accompanied by a due process procedure that would at least allow the student the opportunity to be heard. Fairness to the student would require that he or she be allowed to "make his/her case" in the presence of at least one other person besides the

Daryl Triplett
3DART©

coach or organization sponsor. This other person would preferably be a school administrator. A small formality such as this can save a lot of time, money, and headaches.

Just because a student is off school grounds does not mean they may not be disciplined for actions that negatively impact the school environment and its teachers.

When a student's actions off school grounds reflect negatively on the school, discipline needs to be administered when the student returns to the school environment. This is something which the courts have looked upon favorably. A student who, for example, curses at a teacher at the mall in front of his friends will be subject to discipline when he/she returns to school. To prohibit this type of discipline would diminish the teacher's effectiveness as an authority figure, generally undermine student discipline, and call into question the (moral) direction provided by the school. This means that our responsibilities do not end when students leave the school grounds. The courts have not been very clear in giving schools direction regarding off campus responsibilities, but, at least, they have said that we are not expected to provide constant scrutiny for all students at all times and places. Rather, we must adopt a standard of "reasonableness" when supervising students and ask what a "reasonable," educated person would do in such a situation?

Lockers belong to the school

To avoid problems associated with searches of student lockers, be sure that your board of education adopts a policy which clearly states that lockers are school property and thus are subject to search. This should be included in your student/parent handbook and students and parents should be required to sign a form saying they have read it.

You only need "reasonable suspicion" to conduct a search of a student's belongings

In recent years the courts have given more latitude to educators to conduct searches because of increased problems with violence and drug use in our schools. To search a student's belongings in years past, you had to meet a strict standard of "probable cause" (required for police searches); now, however, a search may be conducted with the much less stringent standard of "reasonable suspicion." This would, for example, allow us to search a student's belongings if he/she is coming out of a restroom and there is smoke in one of the stalls—and it would certainly allow a search if we saw a gun-shaped object in a backpack.

Never conduct a strip search (Except in truly dire circumstances, such as if you feel that the student has something as serious as a bomb in her/his underwear and it is about to explode.)

Conducting strip searches is clearly not the business of school personnel. If you suspect a bomb in a student's underwear, detain him or her and then call the police and the parents. There are indeed horror stories about teachers, especially physical education instructors, who have required all students to strip because someone is missing $5.00 out of their locker. What an opportunity for the lawyers to move in! And, by the way, who is responsible for the supervision and actions of that physical education instructor? You are, Mr. or Ms. Principal!

How you deal with "at risk" students will have a major impact on the reputation and effectiveness of your school

"At risk" students are generally categorized as such because they are economically disadvantaged. Our challenge should be to provide them opportunities at school that will help compensate for those disadvantages. We all must recognize that it is not their fault they are disadvantaged. Providing for such students becomes a greater challenge each year, and the efforts you make in this direction will have a major impact on the effectiveness and reputation of your school. Society's call for greater accountability has led us to rely ever more heavily on various tests/measurements to determine school quality. If your "at risk" students are not properly prepared to perform on these standardized tests, your school will make a poor showing. Encourage your faculty and parents to cooperate in developing programs that will insure that this group of students has opportunities (beyond those of more fortunate students) that will allow them to overcome some of their disadvantages.

Promptly report poor student performance to parents

Regular communication with parents about student performance is an absolute must in today's society, especially when there are problems. Parents need to know the good news as well as the bad news, but delays in reporting bad news can have disastrous results. Use of regular reporting systems like mail-home or take-home forms (with parental signature required) is important, but they should be accompanied by a process of calling or contacting parents early when a grade or conduct problem surfaces. Moreover, if we expect any type of parental assistance in correcting problems, early contact is imperative. "A nickel's worth of prevention is worth a pound of cure" is an old adage, but it may be appropriate here, and is roughly equivalent to the more modern concept of being "pro-active" in relations with parents.

Students learn what they care about

What a difference we could make as educators if we could just internalize the fact that "students learn what they care about" and adjust our programs and instruction accordingly. We are all aware that present day demands for specific types of accountability are putting more pressure on educators to teach specific curricular material, but also that they have given us some latitude in the "how we teach" arena. Educators must determine what students care about, even though it may not be what we care about, and make efforts to incorporate this information into our work with students. We all know this is easier said than done, but we can undoubtedly be more effective if we focus our energies in this direction. In other words, don't teach Shakespeare just because "you ought to know about the writings," but because "it will help you understand social interactions and motivations (very important to teens), and the impact on family relations."

11. CREATING AND MAINTAINING A PRODUCTIVE SCHOOL CLIMATE

There is no quick and simple way to change the atmosphere of a school

If you are a new administrator, changing an existing negative atmosphere in a school may be a real challenge. The best thing you have going for you is that most people would rather work in a pleasant setting and engage in enjoyable interaction with others. You can begin the transformation process by working with a few persons who are concerned and willing to contribute to the development of a positive school climate. This should be at the top of your list because schools that have poor climates are generally academically ineffective. Research points to the importance of the school leader in establishing the tone and climate in the school; also, there is abundant information in the literature about how to improve institutional morale. If you wish to create an effective learning community, a major task will be to develop and maintain high morale in your staff, but remember that "Rome wasn't built in a day."

Create a climate favorable to improvement (an "improvement" culture)

Beyond creating a positive school climate, your challenge should be to establish a culture that respects and encourages improvement. Some schools may be very discouraging places for those who would like to excel, especially for new teachers. Older faculty members may even tell new teachers to "slow down," or call them "brownie noses." Your focus must be on encouraging those who would go the extra mile to produce creative solutions and develop ever better approaches to solving student learning problems. Identify faculty/staff whose attitude is "If it's not broken . . . polish it," then provide recognition and praise for their efforts. An institutional leader needs to be a model for the "improvement" culture, while practicing power sharing and delegation.

Remember that the informal part of your organization (school) is more powerful than the formal; also the culture or norms shared by a group provides powerful forces for molding behavior

We may not like to admit it, but what takes place in informal settings like the "workroom" (never "lounge") is very powerful in determining how others perceive us, and consequently, what sort of actions are taken with respect to us. For an administrator, the best defense in coping with what might be negative perceptions, is to tap into informal channels through staff members who are willing to share their thoughts. When making changes in an organizational setting, it is also important not to overlook the importance and value of normative pressure (e.g. peer pressure), since it can be used to insure the implementation and institutionalization of the changes.

Centralization of authority and formality in procedures generally relate negatively to job satisfaction

There are always those who like formal routines and centralization of authority and feel most comfortable working in such settings. Most of us like to have a clear idea of the parameters and expectations which are attached to our job-related activities; we also like to know about accompanying rewards and punishments. As educated professionals, however, most would like to have a larger degree of autonomy in carrying out our professional activities, and, also, a "slice of the power pie." Modern leaders are recognizing that an autocratic administrative style generally does not produce job satisfaction. Using a democratic approach, and concepts which promote collaboration and empowerment of subordinates, promotes greater organizational effectiveness. Using a "transformational" approach (seeking to transform the goals of the stakeholders into those of the organization as a whole) can also be very effective as the leader promotes collaborative goal setting, shared power and responsibility, and inspires subordinates to rise above self-interest.

Research would indicate that improved job satisfaction may not necessarily result in greater academic productivity, but, given the major problems we are facing with teacher retention, perhaps it could help. Personally, I feel there are other benefits besides improved job satisfaction on the part of teachers (which may not have been thoroughly examined by research) that may ultimately improve student learning.

Try to get everyone involved in an energy conservation program (as part of the school culture)

This suggestion may seem a bit strange, but it has great potential for getting everyone to work together on something they can all agree upon. A united effort of this sort can foster a degree of normative bonding that can carry over into other projects/goals. Faculty involvement might also be enhanced if some rewards could come back to them as a result of the savings on energy. This is a somewhat sad commentary because, given their generally poor financial status, educators are constantly looking for monetary reasons for doing things that should be done just "because they are the right things to do."

12. ACCEPTING CHANGE

People (teachers, etc.) generally don't like change

You have probably heard that "Only babies like changes." This is not always true, but sometimes because of the norms which support the *sta-*

tus quo, it may be necessary to create a certain amount of stress, hopefully as a last resort, to cause people to change/improve. It seems that much of the success (improved student test scores) being experienced with new testing (accountability) programs may be happening because teachers have been stressed by the possibilities of negative consequences if scores did not improve.

If it's not broken . . . polish it!

There are many within our profession who would adopt a different philosophy and would say: "It's working fine just the way it is." "Let's leave well-enough alone." "If it's not broken, don't fix it." Educators should always be looking for better ways to do things. The ". . . polish it" statement, mentioned previously, reflects an attitude that embraces change and a quest for "never ending improvement." You should seek to identify, hire, and nurture staff members who have this kind of improvement "philosophy."

Man's greatest insanity is to see life as it is, not as it should be!

A large, framed picture of a windmill on my wall has guided me on my quest for improvement for many years. Beneath the windmill are the words, "too much sanity may be madness, and the maddest of all, to see life as it is and not as it should be." This quotation relates to Don

Quixote and his quest for a better world in the Man of La Mancha; I feel it should be every educator's credo.

Planned, evolutionary, incremental change is more acceptable to stakeholders than sudden and massive change

Change that can be evolutionary rather than revolutionary has a better chance of being accepted. This is especially true if the stakeholders are involved in the planning and development of the new routine(s) to be adopted and implemented. Major change generally requires long-term, intensive assistance as well as extensive encouragement and facilitation on the part of the administrator.

Teachers need to know the reasons for change

Teachers, like everyone else, want to know "Why are we doing this?" and "What's in it for me?" Too often, leaders pass along directives without explaining that they were handed down from some entity (superintendent, board, state department, etc.) above. The leader should be prepared to answer questions about the need for the change and also to facilitate its acceptance and implementation. The biggest obstacle to the acceptance of change is often the perception, by many, that if we just wait a bit we will probably get new mandates and new direction (from our school board, our legislature, the Federal Government) because this is what teachers have experienced so often in the past. Consequently, there is half-hearted acceptance of many change initiatives, especially those that come from "above."

As agents of change, you must take risks! Be sure, however, that you fully understand the consequences of your actions

If you are going to lead the collective work of improvement in your organization, it will be necessary for you to take risks. Those persons who enter the leadership arena understand that with the "big bucks" (If only that were true!) come greater responsibility and exposure to risk and liability. The fact that you don't want to "fight battles you can't win" should motivate you to gather as much information as you can so you will understand the possible consequences of your risk taking. Remember, you can't make improvements if you are not there. (In other words, it you get fired for trying!)

Just because something didn't work 10 years ago doesn't mean it won't work now

In any profession, there are those who are limited by their level of understanding, lack of insight, and minimal desire to change. The idea that once something (e.g. a new approach, method, program, etc.) has been tried and was not successful, it should be discarded and not considered again, may be prevalent in your organization. But, it precludes the possibility that the new program was not properly implemented because of lack of resources, poorly prepared personnel, etc. Perhaps the idea was ahead of its time or it was the right idea, but put forth at the wrong time or place. Just because it didn't work 10 years ago shouldn't mean it might not work now!

13. FOSTERING EXCELLENCE

Schedule time for teachers to work together

What magic can you perform that will enable teachers, especially those with similar assignments, to have time to work together? Having the same planning time for each department (at the secondary level) may be highly desirable, but it may also be very difficult or impossible to schedule. To see if such an approach would work, start building a schedule (for the secondary level) with no science classes first hour, no math classes second hour, no language arts classes fourth hour, etc. At the elementary level (if you are able to provide a planning time), try to arrange for all third graders to take physical education, music, etc. at the same time so all of these teachers can have this time to work together. Finally, continue using this approach for all grades.

Have an on-going program to keep parents informed about what they can do to help their children (home-learning)

Encourage your teachers (ownership) to develop a program to assist parents as they help their children with home-learning. The type of parental involvement we need most is that which takes place in the home. Just sending kids to school who are "ready to learn" would help a lot.

Use test results as a prescription for re-teaching, changing curriculum, etc.

For years we have given standardized tests and then filed the results in student folders and file cabinets. The scores were just viewed as bits of available information. However, if they are utilized properly, test results should be prescriptive for both teaching and learning. To achieve this, we need to examine test results to determine where students are having problems and then direct specific teaching efforts toward improvement in those areas. In most states, accountability requirements now make it imperative that we use test data in this way to target further instruction.

Make sure there is articulation between grades; also verify that curriculum requirements match those of the tests

How can teachers make sure their course of study meshes with those levels above and below? Is the transition from second to third grade math a smooth one? Are students really prepared to continue into third grade after the end of second grade? The biggest problems seem to occur between grades six and seven where students are changing school sites. Efforts should be coordinated at both the school and district level to insure that students are ready for the next grade or level. Today's accountability initiatives, generally fostered by parents and legislators, demand that we target instruction toward specific curriculum benchmarks or objectives. To some, this is highly desirable, especially if good test results are an important goal, but to others it seems to be limiting, especially if teachers fail to expand their work with students beyond the strict parameters of the required tests. With the assistance of their teachers, administrators must design programs that encourage teaching "beyond the box" and provide incentives, and wherever possible, reward teachers for such efforts.

Develop and maintain an academic focus in your school

One of the components of an "effective school" is an "academic focus." How to demonstrate this? Not just by such "tokenism" as having an annual recognition banquet for scholars, like we have for athletes, but by the priorities we assign to various school activities. Are pep assemblies held during valuable school time? Is the recognition given for athletes or achievement in other activities greater than that provided for academic accomplishment? Is school dismissed for trips to play-off games? Are students allowed to miss classes so they can begin early travel to games, or because they were tired because they got home from their game late last night? Are classes interrupted during testing? Are classes interrupted for matters of administrative convenience? If the answer to any of these questions is "yes," your school is probably lacking an "academic focus."

Academic performance is only one measure of school effectiveness

Even though our reform efforts have basically been directed toward improving test scores of students, we must not lose sight of other qualities we hope to develop in them, qualities not measured by tests. Even though they may not be reflected in accountability programs, we must continue to try to instill in students a sense of right and wrong, of fairness, and respect and compassion for others. We also must ensure they have a sense of the value and dignity of work, an appreciation of beauty, a sense of respect for law, and a wish to become active, contributing members of our society.

We generally don't practice the best that we know

There is abundant research in the field of education (as well as others) that can be useful in helping to improve student learning or related products and services. Unfortunately, much of what has been discovered about effective practice in education has not been incorporated into school life because of constraints on money and time. Political pressures, lack of information, and a general resistance to change may also keep us from applying practices which are "the best that we know." We have, for example, good evidence to support the conclusion that teaching smaller groups of students has academic benefits, but the increased costs associated with smaller classes sometimes prohibit administrators from making major changes in this area.

Even small improvements in student performance may be tough to achieve

Don't get down on yourself or your teachers just because your students don't meet established standards. Some school settings have the best facilities, teaching materials, equipment, curriculum — and teachers working at their absolute best — and students still may not meet standards. This is not to imply that we shouldn't do our best and continue to have high expectations. There is, however, one very important variable that we can't control: The home and the basic life conditions of the children who attend our schools. Again, this is by no means a "cop-out" for educators, but rather a valid reason why school improvement is uniquely difficult to achieve in some situations.

Yourself

1. GENERALLY SPEAKING

Be very visible in your school

Where school administrators are often seen in the hallways and class-rooms, there are generally fewer disciple problems than those where administrators are cloistered in their offices. But, remember, just being seen is not good enough. What are you doing when you are seen? Stop to pick up paper in the hallway, visit with students at their lockers, stand and visit with teachers/students when they are walking between classes, sit in on classes for brief periods, and be sure and attend and participate in all staff development activities. (It upsets teachers when administrators don't attend.)

Turn people on by being enthusiastic yourself

If you expect your teachers to be enthusiastic, you must model enthusiasm. You set the tone for enthusiasm in your school. As Dale Carnegie would say, "Act enthusiastic and you'll be enthusiastic," and hopefully, so will your staff.

People respect you more for "what you are" than "what you do"

We all make mistakes and certainly administrators are no exception. To act as though you never make mistakes, or to blame mistakes on someone else says a lot about "what you are." Indeed, it speaks more loudly than "what you do." What you do is important, but be sure to be gracious and give credit to all of those who have made what you do possible. Let your virtues speak for themselves.

Learn to read body language and control your own

It is very important that you make a conscious effort to understand and effectively use your own body language. What your body language is saying may be very different from the words you are speaking and others can sense this difference. The best way to begin understanding your own body language is to observe and assess the body language of others. Reading a good book on body language or checking out research on the subject can also be very helpful and will give you tips which can help you improve your non-verbal communication skills.

If possible, include yourself in the duty schedule

Teachers appreciate a school leader who is visible (mentioned above), especially one who will include his or her own name on the duty roster. This may not be possible in some situations, but you can win some valuable "acceptance and appreciation points" if you try to do this consistently.

You must be a cheerleader, troubleshooter, and facilitator

The school leader must be the positive person who is always there with encouragement, can solve problems, can fix things (or see that they get fixed), and in general, facilitate the positive and constructive actions of others. When there is an emergency, you must be the one to step forward with a plan and action; you must be the "in charge" person.

As your teachers serve as role models for students, you serve as a role model for teachers (The principal sets to the tone for the school.)

Effective schools research says the principal is the key ingredient in an effective school. If you expect your teachers to be models for students, you must be a model for staff. This means that you will set the standard for dress, democratic action, compassion, morality, scholarship, professionalism, etc. It is difficult to "make a silk purse out of a sow's ear," but I am confident all of you are somewhere above a sow's ear in terms of intellect and ability. At the same time, this does indeed mean that you should acknowledge, at least to yourself, your weaknesses and work to improve them.

Look for hidden agendas/curricula in your school

Are there things going on in your school such as hidden agendas or even hidden curricula? These can often go undetected by administration and can be very destructive to students and even staff. As a principal, I was once very surprised to find that all of my freshmen boys were undergoing humiliating initiation experiences. The initiations had been going on for several years and were conducted by the seniors during school hours and on school grounds. This type of agenda was probably not nearly as harmful as some that may encourage bigotry, racism, or sexism. Sometimes these may become a part of a curriculum for one or more teachers. If such situations exist at your school, it is your responsibility to uncover them and make sure they are ended. The best way to find out about such activities is probably through being in the "loop" as far as informal communication is concerned. Often, staff members are willing to share such information informally, especially if they feel it will benefit them, you, or the organization.

You don't get a second chance to make a good first impression, but . . .

If the first impression you make on someone happens to be negative, let's hope you get the chance to change it. Likewise, you should give others a chance to make a good second impression ("Do unto others . . .").

Avoid saying "I" did . . .

Even if you were the person responsible for some school success, surely you had others who were very instrumental in the accomplishment. Even though it is very tempting to take all the credit, avoid saying "I" did . . . and say "our school did . . . ," "members of our faculty did . . . ," "our support staff did . . ." The rewards for such unselfishness will come back to you many times over.

Successful leaders have strong positive beliefs in the abilities of their employees

Douglas McGregor's theories make a lot of sense, especially in initial interaction with your staff members. If your perceptions of any of them are negative, you are probably going to interact with them in a negative way. Their reaction will probably also be negative—a sort of "Pygmalion phenomenon" where perceptions and treatment engender like responses and vice-versa. The wisest approach for a leader is to find the good qualities and abilities in those you supervise and build on these. It is especially important for you as a new leader to exhibit acceptance of staff and their abilities, while, at the same time, acknowledging to yourself, that there are undoubtedly areas that need improvement. There will always be those who will need individual guidance, admonitions, and even correction, but to get "the best" out of everyone, accentuate the positive and praise effort and accomplishment.

Keep an open mind; discuss, don't argue

You may disagree with someone, but practice not being disagreeable when you do. Be sure to listen carefully and make it a habit to ask for more information and clarification before you react. Try to "put yourself in the other person's shoes" to better understand their point of view.

What to do when someone criticizes you

When someone criticizes you, ask yourself if there was any truth to what was said, if so, make changes. If there is none, ignore the criticism and live in such as way that no one will believe the negative remark.

Cultivate a sense of humor

A sense of humor is very import for administrators. Those administrators who are not able to laugh at/in many of the situations we encounter in schools will find that their daily work is more physically and mentally exhausting than those who do. Laughter is often the shortest distance between two people. It also aids digestion! There are many situations where a little humor can serve to effectively ease tension.

Arrive early

Arriving early may be a tough assignment, but it is very important and has many rewards. Remember that you are a model and you are also the cheerleader, troubleshooter, etc. Arriving early allows you to make sure things will run smoothly and gives you a chance to visit and get acquainted with people on a relaxed basis. Hurriedly rushing in at the last minute, or even late, makes others wonder about your organizational skills and effectiveness.

Play fair

Teachers "like" principals to be considerate, but they also want them to be consistent about upholding rules and applying them to everyone without exception. Don't play favorites.

Be an active listener

Being an active listener may take some practice, but it will be worth the effort. If you expect to nurture others' enthusiasm and respect for you as a listener, you must show your interest in other's ideas, proposals, etc. This means you must give your undivided attention (wherever possible) to the person who is addressing you, make eye contact, and provide affirmation through nodding, smiling, etc. Repeating or paraphrasing what the other person has said is also effective. e.g. "This is what I hear you are saying . . .", or "Did you mean this or something else?" You should also make sure you are not displaying any negative body language (such as your arms folded across your chest).

Don't try to make everyone into a clone of yourself

Just because you tend to be a type "A" personality doesn't mean everyone will be or should be like you. Differences in personal styles are highly desirable and it is important to be able to understand and appreciate them. It may be difficult at times to understand why some do not have the organizational skills you possess and especially why they can't get required reports in on time. Again, look for the positive qualities these individuals have and give them support as needed.

Different approaches to leadership may be required in various situations

Even though democratic or participative leadership is generally the most effective approach, there are times when you must be autocratic with staff members (we would hope this would be a rarity) and others. Consider what might be necessary with young children. If they have wandered into the street, you would likely say to them "Get out of the street, now!"—and not "Would you like to get out of the street?" Conversely, a *laissez-faire* (hands off) approach may even be most appropriate if you are leading a group of highly professional, goal-oriented people. Your best approach may be to get out of the way, offer encouragement, and merely facilitate their actions. The challenge you face is to determine when the situation dictates that you be authoritarian (perhaps, with young teachers who may need more direction and clearly defined responsibilities), when to be democratic, and when to just stand back and be the cheerleader.

Everyone wants to be loved, including you

Of course, this is an overstatement and "loved" is probably not the correct word. Most of us seek the approval and acceptance from others and our actions are often influenced by this need. Even though administrators have this same need, they must not allow it to influence them when making difficult decisions; this is a pretty big order and one that many cannot fulfill. Effective leaders/administrators must be able to put this need aside when working with staff members who may occasionally need to be admonished. They must also learn that there are definitely times when they must say "no," even though saying "no" may cause you not to be "loved," it may garner the respect you deserve.

Before you pass information to others, ask yourself three things about what you are planning to say: (1) Is it true? (2) Is it kind? (3) Is it necessary?

This advice applies especially to informal communication, and it is something which should be shared with staff members on a regular basis. Above all, the administrator should always follow his or her own advice.

2. PERCEPTIONS

Remember that people's perceptions are real (to them) and they respond in keeping with these perceptions.

There is probably not much by way of positive correlation between how leaders say they behave and the way subordinates see them actually behaving. Our perceptions are our reality and our actions/behaviors are determined by these perceptions. How are you perceived? How can you find out? It is very important to recognize that the way you perceive something may be very different from the way it is perceived by others. Your experiences, and perhaps even your ego, have created a sort of filter through which you look at the world. It would not be unusual to find that a principal would give herself an "A" for "effectiveness as a disciplinarian" whereas the faculty would collectively give a her "C." Who is most nearly correct is not important. What is important is that the faculty will react to you based on their perceptions, not yours.

Do you have too many rules and regulations?

Many teachers feel that we have too many rules and regulations. Unfortunately, our legal system has caused them to proliferate. Today's administrators and teachers are best served by rules and regulations which clearly delineate our responses to problems in such areas as treatment of special students, discipline, and student rights in general. Ask yourself and your staff if there are rules which you could do without.

Daryl Triplett
3-DART©

3. DECISION MAKING/PROBLEM SOLVING

**Remember that "facts" culled from research
are not as important as the general patterns they reveal
and the explanations they provide.**

Some of us tend to get "hung up" on what we interpret as "facts" extracted from research, especially when these "facts" don't fit properly into our unique situation, and we find ourselves having to say "it didn't work for us." Unlike research in the sciences, research in education is very difficult in that there are many uncontrollable variables. This means that we cannot generalize the findings—they may be relative to one group, but that cannot be extended to other groups or situations because each may be different in many ways. Even though the results of a piece of research may not be totally applicable to our situation, it is important that we do not disregard, but consider possible implications for our situation. We may find bits of specific information or general patterns that provide explanations and guide us in our efforts to improve programs or skills.

When confronted with a problem, huddle, stall a bit

When confronted with a problem that doesn't need immediate response, make it your practice to "buy yourself some time." We

all can make better decisions when we have time to get more information.

Insist that, when teachers come to you with their problems, they also bring you a possible solution

Challenge your staff members to use their problem solving abilities by requiring that, when they come to you with problems, they also bring possible solutions. Some teachers are prone to dropping all of their problems right on the principal's desk without first using their own resources to solve them. If you require that they bring possible solutions, then responsibility is immediately shared. The work you do together can be seen as an empowering activity when the "possible solution" becomes the one you implement. (This was worth mentioning a second time!)

Problems rarely come to us at the point of their inception

Unfortunately, when administrators first encounter a problem it is often already in "full bloom." Acknowledging this fact means we must be diligent in our proactive efforts to anticipate problem areas and put preventive strategies in place. It also accentuates the need to be "out and about" and very visible to students and staff.

There is no "best way" to solve a problem

Problems come in all sizes and shapes and the best solution in one situation may prove to be a poor one for a similar situation. The best solutions are the result of considering all the pertinent information about a problem in a calm, unemotional way. The more information you can obtain, generally the better your decision or solution. Often it is desirable to draw upon the best insights of others in assessing problems and seeking solutions to them. It is also important to remember that if the solution was not effective the first time it probably won't be the second time. If the first paddling didn't stop the misbehavior, the second or third paddling will likely be doled out for the purpose of personal gratification, or for some other inappropriate reason. Good policies and procedures which result from collaborative efforts can be a great help in solving problems, but, above all, in avoiding them in the first place. Finally, if policies and procedures are to remain effective, they need to be evaluated and revised on a regular basis, probably yearly.

Determine the "right thing to do" and then "just do it!"

School administrators are not often blessed with extra time to consider options and strategies; often, they must act quickly. This fact will probably not change soon and it makes it all the more important that we determine the "right things to do." It also implies that we can't do everything at the same time; we must select what is most important at a given time and do it right. If we put too much "on our plate" a good deal of our efforts will end up "half-baked" and will reflect negatively on ourselves and others.

Although we expect ethical behavior, especially from professionals, there may be disagreement about what is ethical

Our standards for ethical behavior are greatly influenced by our past experiences. Often our standards have taken root in us as a result of religious background, or they have been molded by parents. In my later years, my own somewhat rigid concept of ethical behavior has been altered as I have come to understand that perceptions of the same situation differ from individual to individual. What may be moral or ethical for me may be immoral or unethical for someone else because of their past experiences and their ethical perceptions. Fortunately, the teaching profession and most professional school administrator groups have adopted professional standards for ethical behavior. These standards are fairly general and are probably very acceptable to those within these groups. The real problems arise when situations we encounter do not fall within the scope of these standards.

Please consider a concept which may appear to be less than ethical, but nevertheless, deserves examination, namely that of "the greater good." Often, we find we must ask ourselves "Is the greater good being served by my action?" What if, as a superintendent, you are asked by a board member to recommend the firing of several teachers. You are told you will lose your job if you do not make the recommendation. You know the unethical board member is very powerful and can easily garner all the board votes needed to fire the teachers or yourself. What the board member has said to you has been told to you in private and you have no proof it was ever said. You have been very successful in your new job; your empowering leadership style has caused your teachers to be enthusiastic and hard working and students are making great academic improvement. You have recently purchased a beautiful home and your spouse has a good job. Should you prepare to recommend the terminations of the teachers? What if it was requested that you recommend the termination of only one teacher and not several?

4. USE OF TIME

Don't disturb teachers with the intercom; keep all interruptions to a minimum

In cases of emergency, it may be necessary to interrupt, but please consider alternatives that will not disturb the teacher and students!!!

Stand up behind your desk for short meetings

When you are pressed for time it is important that you have a polite strategy for keeping meetings short. When a staff member enters and wants to talk about something which is of little importance (This is guaranteed to happen!), stand up behind your desk for the discussion and don't invite them to sit down. If that doesn't work, come around from behind your desk and slowly walk the person to the door. You can generally invite them to make an appointment to see you at a later point, and, in the meantime, request relevant information or materials in advance of that meeting. Alternatively, you might ask your secretary to interrupt you after a specified time period.

"Quality" time on task doesn't just happen

We can all improve on the way we use our time. An important topic for professional development activities, in which everyone can participate, including you, would be time management. Do everything possible to provide for student/teacher "time on task" and to create a culture in which there is the clear expectation that time will be used wisely.

Managing your time really means managing yourself

Effective time management for your organization has to begin with you. If you know your time-use skills are poor, then you must set about to improve them. It is generally best to work with a group of several people who have similar problems and to exchange information about how each of you is going about your day, your successes, and failures. There is ample literature on the internet or elsewhere that can give you ideas on ways to improve.

Don't have an open door policy

One of the biggest time wasters is an open door policy. Many pride themselves on saying "I am always available when you need me." But, what if a visitor just wants to "kill time" with idle "chit chat?" Of course, it goes without saying that you should always be available for important discussions and emergencies, but it is also advisable to ensure (or at least try to) that you have blocks of uninterrupted time for your own work. You should let your staff know that you will generally have your door shut during certain times to make phone calls, or when you need to do paper work, or any sort of thoughtful assessment and planning, etc.

Use "to do" lists

Today's administrators are extremely busy, *if* they are doing their jobs properly, and it is not easy to remember everything that needs attention and to set clear priorities. "To do" lists, in whatever form you wish to make them, are essential for effective administration. A large desk calendar is often useful for this task, since you can jot down notes and times for meetings, etc. and maintain a daily perspective at a glance. A pocket calendar with space for notes can also be very helpful, as can an electronic organizer. The latter are compact and can hold very large amounts of information. Also recommended is the use of lists of things to be done on a daily or weekly basis. These are best kept on your desk for easy access and viewing. Time management gurus would advise ranking the items on your list in order of their relative importance and concentrating on the most important one until it is completed. This approach doesn't always work well, particularly for those administrators who prefer to work on items which fit into available blocks of time. Marking off and dating the items as they are completed provides a sense of accomplishment and a record of your activities. These "to do" lists should be filed (perhaps in a "done" file for future reference) when a new list is created. Completed lists can be valuable for "C.Y.R." ("cover your rear") purposes and can also help to reconstruct a record of your activities. Most of the time there will be a number of items on the list which have not been completed; these need to be carried over to the new list.

The telephone and drop-in visits are great time wasters

Effective time management skills would dictate that you have and execute a plan for answering phone calls, and for reducing the number and duration of drop-in visits, especially when they are for social reasons. An effective way to respond to non-emergency phone calls is to allocate at least two time periods in the course of the day during which you return calls. Your secretary can inform callers that you will be returning the call between 10:30-11:00, (for calls received in the morning), and between 2:30-3:00 (for those received in the afternoon). Your secretary should also ask callers if their request could be addressed by someone other than the principal, and/or ask them to leave a message.

Remember that it is important that you always have some time when your door is closed. But even when it is open, you still need to implement certain strategies to protect your time. If you can sense that an uninvited visitor would like to stay and talk, rise from your desk and slowly proceed to the door as you converse. If you are busy but need to talk with an individual, tell them you are trying to meet a deadline but you want to talk with them. Ask them to make an appointment with your secretary. When your staff understands that you are serious about using your school time wisely, they will respect your needs and a lot of the social-type visits will end. It is important that you maintain pleasant social relations with your staff, but they shouldn't detract from your effectiveness. A good time to visit informally with staff and students is when you are in the halls, before, during, and after school (when you are being "visible").

5. CONFLICT AND STRESS

Events or happenings do not have to upset human beings

Administrators are not expected to be emotionless, but they are expected to be models for others, and provide organization and stability where it is needed. It is important that we understand that an event or happening does not have to be upsetting; rather, it is we who upset ourselves by our thoughts about such things. We must be concerned about the example we provide, especially in a time of crisis.

Learn to tell the difference between battles and wars. Don't fight the ones you can't win

My definition of a "battle" is "a conflict of short duration where a major personal investment, relative to one's ethical and philosophical principles, has not been made." In other words, you can lose without sacrificing such principles, and also without damaging your future ability to provide effective, ethical leadership. You should expect to loose a number of battles, probably daily. There are definitely times when you should retreat and save your resolve and resources for another day. There are also times when you should retire altogether from a situation, hopefully gracefully, and "cut your loses." When the school attorney advises you that your efforts to terminate an insubordinate teacher will probably be for naught because you have failed to adequately document the issues, it is time to back off and begin a process of better documentation.

"Wars," on the other hand, represent major challenges to our core beliefs about right and wrong. It is important that you don't do anything that would cause "battles" to escalate into "wars" because the stakes are much higher. People are often willing to compromise in an effort to extinguish the fires of battle, but "wars" generally have winners and losers and the aftermath of them may be as traumatic as the conflict itself. Before you engage in a "war," be clear on the fact that you cannot, in good faith, "give in" on your principles. A word of warning: If you do have to go to "war" against unprincipled groups of influential parents who have an axe to grind, your neck may be the one that feels the blade. Board members are often influenced by constituents, especially if they are elected by those same persons. So, before you enter the fray, make sure you are well-prepared and have adequate support from those who will determine the outcome of your employment situation.

Choose your battle site wisely!

You can't win a battle in the hallway. If you choose to engage in one in front of others, you will generally be the loser. It may appear that you have won because the opponent yielded to you as school principal, but, in the eyes of observers, you have probably diminished your status by allowing yourself to be drawn into such a public scenario. There are always those who will take the side of the "underdog" regardless of whether they are right or wrong, especially if your attack was not controlled and professional. There are also times when you will need to choose whether a battle should take place in your office or on your opponent's turf. Generally speaking, if you want to appear conciliatory and non-threatening, you might offer to meet somewhere other than

your office. If the tenor of the meeting is expected to be heated, and appears it might be necessary to use your power as principal, plan to have it in your office with witnesses close by. It is also a good idea to have your tape recorder ready.

Build on similarities rather than differences

To avoid "battles" and "wars" you need to have certain strategies readily available. Building on similarities rather than differences can be a starting point for compromise or for diffusing a situation that could become explosive. You must maintain a cool head when confronted with a possible conflict situation and quickly sort through those items which can reveal similarities in beliefs, knowledge, backgrounds, etc. If two parents confront you in your office about concerns they have about the amount of homework their child is being assigned, after listening carefully to their position, it might be good to first thank them for being interested parents. You might then explain that you are also the parent of a teenager and also concerned about the amount of time being spent on homework. Then, you might begin explaining about the new pressures for higher student scores required for college entrance and the faculty's response to it, namely, to ask students to do more at home.

Remember, the absence of stress is death

Stress keeps us going, but, ultimately, it may be what causes us to change. The key is to understand how to use stress constructively in our lives and the lives of others. There are many who feel very

comfortable with the status quo and will not change unless some pressure is applied. While it is an administrator's job to maintain balance in an organization, merely maintaining the status quo is not a desirable goal. Leaders often need to subject others in the organization to stresses which may positively influence their performance and productivity. Consider the case where an employee receives a negative performance evaluation. Hopefully this will cause his or her performance to improve. The evaluator may not enjoy giving such an evaluation, but it should have a positive and constructive purpose.

Often the stress to improve performance comes from outside the organization/school. The administrator is charged with maintaining overall balance but is also held accountable for the performance of the staff. When the state or school board issues new regulations or accountability requirements, the school must comply. To keep stresses of this sort from being overwhelming and counterproductive, the new regulations or accountability requirements must be addressed by the faculty collectively. The principal must then facilitate the development of plans for adherence to the requirements and accomplishment of revised goals. This kind of approach allows faculty members to know "it is not the principal's fault," and also allows them to have a degree of ownership, as stakeholders in the plan(s) to be implemented.

Forget about counting to 10

If necessary, count to 1,000 before doing or saying something that could make matters worse.

Getting upset won't help

You must be in control of yourself. When you let other people or situations cause you to "lose your cool," you reduce your ability to function effectively. Part of the solution to this is recognizing that this sort of thing is potentially a problem for you. If you have a problem with your emotions, it is time for you to begin developing strategies for maintaining personal control.

If nobody else heard it, it didn't happen

If a parent or teacher says undesirable things to you in the privacy of your office, you may not like it but you have no evidence that it even happened. (That is unless you had your tape recorder running, and then it probably wouldn't have been said.) Of course you don't like others to raise their voices to you or to call you names, but remember "Getting upset won't help." Now may be the time to count to 1000. You must have thick skin, and, like it or not, people will not always be courteous to you or treat you with special respect just because you are an administrator.

No sarcasm or personal attacks please!

Sarcasm or personal attacks should not be a part of the arsenal available to you for personal defense. "Do unto others. . . ." It is of special importance that you never use sarcasm or personal attacks when others may be observing. Negative remarks or attacks only diminish you and your potential for effectiveness in the eyes of observers, even if they seem warranted.

6. C.Y.R. (COVER YOUR REAR)

Have a tape recorder on your desk and ready to go in a hostile situation

An angry Mrs. Smith has just entered your office and a string of profanity has been directed at you and one of your staff members. Your first words should probably be: "I record all of these proceedings; today is Oct. 16, Mrs. Smith is here to discuss. . . ." A good quality tape recorder should cost you less than $50.00. It should be on your desk and plugged up and ready to go at all times. The presence of the recorder will discourage a verbal attack and what is recorded could be valuable if civil litigation or criminal action is necessary.

Keep your ducks in a line. Document, document, document!

Be pro-active by making sure information which could relate to a conflict situation is well-organized and well-documented. Keep good notes

relative to situations which have the potential to blossom into battles or even wars. Have signed witnesses to those discussions or conferences in which a disagreement or conflict occurred. It may be necessary to use these witnesses and your documentation in grievances, due process, or legal proceedings. Ideally, if your documentation is of sufficient quantity and quality, you will never have to use it.

Make sure teachers are on duty when they are supposed to be

Much of the litigation which is encountered by teachers and administrators relates to inadequate supervision. It is the administrator's responsibility to assure that students are safe when they are at school; this means providing appropriate supervision at all times. If a student is injured when a teacher is not performing an assigned duty, like playground supervision, the principal will be held responsible, along with the teacher, because it is the principal's responsibility to see that teachers are on duty as scheduled. This is an area which needs special attention in many schools.

There is another reason why principals should make sure teachers are on duty when and where they are assigned, namely, staff morale. Teachers who are performing the duties assigned to them, do not like to absorb the responsibilities of those who are not. They also know it is the administrator's responsibility to see that the duty schedule is developed and monitored fairly. If this is not happening, they have negative feelings toward the administrator and about the lack of courage that this demonstrates, and his or her ability to treat everyone fairly. And, they tend not only to judge harshly in one situation, but to judge other incidents in this way as well.

React immediately when you are notified of a situation which may be hazardous to students. It is your responsibility to provide a safe environment for your students and staff. This means reacting quickly when you are notified of a situation that may be hazardous. It may also mean acting outside the limits of existing procedures or policy to correct a problem. If the hazard necessitates evacuating the building, or moving students to other areas, you should do so without hesitation. If it is something related to repairs or maintenance, you should immediately notify the persons responsible for such and document your contact. It may still be necessary that you move students or make other changes to provide a safe environment. You will be forgiven if you take extraordinary precautions to protect students and staff, but not if you fail to act. For minor repairs of items which may become hazards, be sure to submit appropriate requests and document, document, document. It is also a good idea to give a copy of your submitted request to any teacher who may have called your attention to the needed repair.

7. POLITICS/PUBLIC RELATIONS

Keep your building clean; also make sure the exterior looks good

If the appearance of a building isn't a major concern to you, acknowledge that it may be important to others. The appearance of your building and facilities makes a strong statement to those who pass by and those who enter. In addition to working to ensure that the school makes a good impression during the academic year, it is very important to have a summertime maintenance program which keeps the building and grounds groomed. The building committee, discussed earlier, may be of real value here. An organized effort by parents, faculty, and students could make substantial improvement in the appearance of your facilities and it would probably be a good idea for others to see you getting your hands dirty in a Saturday morning school improvement effort.

Don't fight the media! (They buy their ink by the barrel.)

The media can be our best friend or our worst nightmare. The best approach to working with the media is to be candid and responsive to their requests. It is a good practice to maintain a cordial relationship with those who can help or hurt your school very easily. Utilizing the resources of a news staff can also offer benefits beyond the immediate need to have an information resource available for students and classes. If a news entity, like a radio station, becomes a frequent visitor to your school and its classrooms, it is most likely going to be supportive.

Change the name of your "lounge" to "workroom"

What do people do in "lounges?" The general perception of such places is probably that it is a relaxing area where people may be having a cocktail and a cigarette. That isn't exactly what goes on in these areas in our schools, so surely a different name might be more appropriate. It is my strong suggestion that you immediately remove the "lounge" sign and install one that says "workroom." Most would like to think that we are working, even when we are not directly supervising students. Some of our citizens are critical of educators because they believe we have short workdays, only teach 8 or 9 months, and have all sorts of vacations. Surely we don't want to give them more fuel for their fires by spending part of our day in a "lounge."

Winning teams and organizations can foster other successful school endeavors

Winning teams and successful organizations create a school and community environment that helps us operate our schools more successfully. It is great to be blessed with programs and teams that are outstanding, but such programs are the result of hard work and dedication on the part of teachers and their students. Appropriate recognition and nurturing of these efforts can stimulate success in other programs. Administrators should be aware that good community feelings about successful programs can also have major ramifications relative to school tax support levies and building construction initiatives. Passing a bond issue is generally much easier when you have just completed a winning football season, and even better if you are state champions.

Make your words soft and tender today, because tomorrow you may have to eat them!

This old saying can keep you out of a lot of trouble. It implies that you should be a good listener and suspend judgment until you get more information. When Mrs. Jones was late getting her report into the office, you may have wanted to tell her to "shape up," until you found out that her father had passed away the day before, and she and been at the hospital and then had to make funeral arrangements because she had no mother and was the only child.

Learn to use qualifying phrases like "generally speaking," "in my opinion," and "it has been my experience"

This can save you a lot of embarrassment. When you use such modifiers, you are leaving yourself some "wiggle room." It is also true, in education especially, that there is not much we can say with great certainty. If you lace your discussion with such terms, you may also be perceived by others as less dogmatic and not authoritarian.

White lies may be appropriate at times

One of the Ten Commandments (No, they are not "suggestions.") tells us that we should not "bear false witness." But, the New Testament tells us we should love our neighbor as we love our self (Do unto others. . .). Think about it for a moment. Are there times when you would rather be "spared the truth"? If someone invites you to some event (perhaps an art show) and you are tired and really don't

like art shows, you might say you have another obligation. This generally satisfies the other person, they don't feel hurt, and a positive relationship is maintained. Do you think someone really wants to hear about all of your aches, pains, and troubles when they ask you "How are you doing?"? When your white lies are used for good purposes and are designed not to hurt others, my guess is that you will be forgiven.

Members of your support staff can be the organization's worst enemies, or its best promoters

Don't underestimate the power of your support staff to help promote your organization. In most schools, and many other types of organizations, these persons are neither valued nor treated as if their contributions mattered. This is an area where a few small changes can result in greater effectiveness and efficiency. Often these persons may feel no cultural or normative attachment to the organization and thus do not hesitate to take negative messages to the community. Apart from receiving many types of informal recognition, these persons should be invited to all staff/teacher meetings. What they have to say in such meetings should be seriously considered. They should be included in committees like other staff members. Everything that can be done to make them feel like valued members of the organization should be done. When they feel that their contributions are respected, their performance will improve and they will also be "good will" ambassadors for the organization. This is the sort of thing that can "happen" as a result of a positive inclusion program. The results may not always be optimal, but the benefits make it well-worth the effort, however small they may be.

Your secretary has more contact with the public than you do

In many instances your patrons will be better acquainted with your secretary than they are with you; this is especially true in schools. If you can acknowledge that this is the case, it becomes very important to make sure that person is a positive reflection on the school and also upon yourself. You may need to do some type of informal assessment

Daryl Triplett
3D ART©

to determine how that person relates to callers and visitors. If you do such an assessment and it indicates that he or she is making an unpleasant or unprofessional impression, you must immediately begin work on changing this. If that person is not able to make needed changes, you must make the difficult choice to replace him or her with someone one who has the right qualities for the position. A compassionate approach is a necessity in this situation, but it is also imperative that the person who fills this job be competent, friendly, helpful, and present an image which reflects positively on the school.

Make yourself available to community groups as a spokesman for your school and for education in general

Even if you are not the world's greatest speaker, it is very important that you let your community know you are available and ready to speak to all sorts of groups. If you don't feel comfortable making speeches, suggest a format that includes discussion and informal commentary. In general, the more engagements you have the more comfortable you will become with public speaking. When you make these talks, be sure you are armed with the latest information about your school and be prepared with positive anecdotes about school happenings. It is also important that you offer praise and recognition for special accomplishments of staff members. Keep in mind that the praise and recognition you give to others (even when you have been very instrumental in bringing about the good things which have happened), will return to you many times over. Taking teachers or outstanding students along with you to such public meetings (wherever possible) is also desirable.

8. FINANCE

Have a purpose when you do a fundraiser

Never raise funds just to be raising funds. The most successful fund raisers have clearly-stated, highly laudable purposes. A parent/teacher organization can get energized over a project to raise funds to buy a set of encyclopedias (Our goal is $16,800; $560 per set for 30 classrooms.) for each classroom or new curtains for the stage ($12,900 installed). If you are raising funds so teachers can attend seminars or workshops, this should be clearly stated as well. Perhaps your fundraiser could be for multiple purposes: workshop expenses, computer software for the computer lab, and funding for the spring honors banquet.

Make sure to have the financial accounts audited before you begin as a new principal

When principals lose their jobs it is often because of financial issues. To provide some protection, when you begin as principal in a new position, it is very important that you have the school's finances examined. It would be most desirable to have the accounts examined by the district's auditors. If such an audit is not feasible, an examination could be performed by the district's finance officer or business manager. This proactive approach protects you from blame for poor accounting or other financial problems that were generated by the prior administration.

Make sure two people count the money

You would think that a policy that required two people to count money received from gates, concessions, etc. would be in place in all districts. Unfortunately, principals are often without district policies and procedures to guide their activities in the financial arena. Good/safe practice would dictate that two persons would count money, in the presence of each other, and record the results of their counting for comparisons. If the results are not the same, recounts are necessary. It is also important that organizational sponsors (pepclub, band, etc.) count all money before it is given to the secretary for counting and deposit. The secretary should also count the money, making sure her total was the same, and give a receipt to the sponsor. These procedures will help provide individual accountability and insure there is proper accounting and utilization of school monies.

Use numbered tickets (always)

Numbered tickets should be used anytime admission is charged at a school event. The beginning ticket numbers should be recorded. When the event is completed and money is being counted (again, by two people), the amount of the proceeds should equal the number of tickets sold multiplied by the admission price. This would seem to be good common sense and a matter of policy, but, unfortunately, it is not always the practice.

Receipt all monies received

Receipts should be given for all monies received by the office. It is best to have a numbered receipt book, for audit/tracking purposes. Carbon or duplicate copies should be made of each receipt issued.

Avoid keeping a slush fund;
record all receipts and expenditures

Keeping money from the pop machine and concession sales in a cigar box (or some similar receptacle) in the school safe is poor practice and leaves room for abuse and suspicion about the disposition of such funds. When the money is taken from the pop machine it should be counted, receipted, and prepared for deposit in the school bank account. If you maintain a petty cash fund, it should be separate from these funds, and all expenditures should be documented with receipts. Best practice would use checks, even for small financial transactions.

Remember the Golden Rule: "He who has the gold, rules!"

Be nice to the business manager or the one who holds the purse strings. It is a well-known that most school principals and teachers feel there are

never enough funds to adequately finance school operations (special programs, supplies, professional development, etc.), especially from the central office. It is also important to acknowledge that "The squeaky wheel gets the grease," at least most of the time. Make sure your needs are known by the business manager and the rationale for your needed funds is well-documented. Often administrators do not receive what they need because they do not ask. Your faculty will appreciate your efforts to obtain funds, especially when they are fruitful.

When all else fails, read the directions

What more can be said?

FINAL THOUGHTS

From whence all of the thoughts listed here came, I'm not sure. Some of them are mine and some belong to unnamed others, but they offer guidance, reflection, inspiration, and perhaps a bit of humor.

1. It's what we think we know that often prevents us from learning.
2. Every great achievement was once considered impossible.
3. The best time to plant a tree was 20 or 30 years ago, the next best time is today.
4. I'm doing the best I can, but I'll get better.
5. It can't be done, but I'll try.
6. Sometime I say things I haven't even thought of yet, but I'm working on it.
7. I know what to do, I just don't know where to start.
8. Things remain the same because we want them to.
9. Don't let dollars determine who can or can't be a cheerleader.
10. Everyone wants to be loved.
11. Students can't learn if they aren't there.
12. Keep your tape recorder on your desk and ready to roll.
13. Involve your teachers in screening and selecting staff.
14. Make sure teachers are on duty.
15. Cats may not eat gym suits, but they may mess on homework.
16. Buy your booze somewhere else. (This is for administrators who live in small communities.)
17. Don't beat the teachers out the doors after school. (And don't let the teachers beat the students out the door.)
18. Make sure that all students, except those who are being disciplined, get to attend any school-sponsored event; even if they don't have their dollar.
19. Field trips must always relate to a legitimate school or classroom objective.
20. A Bandaid on the big toe won't cure lung cancer. (It seems like a lot of our initiatives to improve education are like this.)
21. Always leave it cleaner than you found it.
22. The shortest distance between two points is not on the grass. (Remember, you are a model.)

23. If you find yourself in a hole, the first thing you do is stop digging. (Rogers)
24. Never miss a good chance to shut up. (Rogers)
25. It doesn't take a genius to spot a goat in a flock of sheep.
26. Few people are successful unless a lot of other people want them to be. (Brower)
27. You don't lead by hitting people over the head, that is battery, not leadership. (Eisenhower)
28. A hard day's work gives promise of a good night's rest.
29. It didn't work then, but it may work now.
30. When a hammer is the only tool you have in your tool box, everything looks like a nail.
31. Don't try to teach a pig to sing; it wastes your time and irritates the pig.
32. The more we delay in meeting reasonable demands, the more unreasonable they become.
33. To try where there is little hope is to risk failure. Not to try guarantees it.
34. When you can't see a light at the end of the tunnel; go down there and light a candle.
35. Let us put our minds together and see what we can create for our children.
    (Sitting Bull)

References

Herzberg, F., "One More Time: How Do You Motivate Employees?" *Harvard Business Review* 46 (1968): 53.

Maslow, A. H., (1954) *Motivations and Personality*. New York: Harper and Row.

Index

About the Author

During his 40 plus years as an educator, Dr. LoVette has served in a variety of positions. Beginning his teaching career in 1963, after receiving his Master of Science degree in education from Kansas State Teachers College, he taught science and was intramural director at Atchison High School in Atchison, Kansas. After teaching botany, zoology, and general science for 3 years he returned to Emporia to work on a Specialist Degree in Educational Administration. During the next two years he worked closely with Dr. Marvin Schadt (whom he considers a mentor) as he learned about the roles and responsibilities of school administrators. LoVette assisted Dr. Schadt and other faculty with school improvement surveys, visited numerous student teachers, assisted with masters' theses, and was hired the second year (after completing the Educational Specialist) as an instructor. His major responsibilities as an instructor in the Education Department were visiting student teachers in eastern Kansas and teaching several courses

In 1968 Dr. LoVette took his first administrative position as principal in Conway Springs, Kansas, serving as principal for grades 7–12 for 3 years. Those years were filled with both rewarding and trying experiences. LoVette, at the age of 27, was young for an administrator and this was the beginning of the "70's" and all that might be implied related to student rights movements.

In 1971, LoVette took a position as Administrative Assistant in the College of Engineering at Oklahoma State University while he worked on his doctorate in Educational Administration. Completing his degree in 1973, under the able direction of Dr. Kenneth St. Clair (whom he also considers a mentor), he took an administrative position in a community college. This was quite a departure from his originally planned development, but he loved the job and served 5 years as Dean of Student Services at Cowley County Community College/Area Vocational Technical School. He also served as Athletic Director for several very successful programs during this time.

In 1978, Dr. LoVette returned to the K–12 scene as Superintendent of Schools at Eudora, Kansas. After 5 years, working with a dedicated School Board and staff, he decided to move to a larger district and was hired as Superintendent in McAlester, Oklahoma where he served for 2 years (1983–85). His experience during those 2 years involved closing an old high school and implementing a new facility and staffing plan that required the relocating of over 30 staff members. When he left the district's cash balance had increased from about $300,000 to approximately $1,300,000. Needless to say, the turmoil created by the staffing changes, school closing, and economy measures necessitated that he find another position.

During the 1985–86 school year, Dr. LoVette served the Fort Worth schools as a Research Consultant and assisted with research in the schools. During that time he was searching for another superintendent's position. He was hired by the Gering, Nebraska schools in 1986, as Superintendent. His wife, Senna, also an experienced educator and former administrator, was unable to find a teaching position (district policy did not permit her to be employed where her husband was an administrator) and consequently, after two years they left for another superintendent's position where she could be employed as a teacher. His experience in Nebraska was very positive and he observed that the School Board always acted professionally.

He then moved to Tahlequah, Oklahoma (Capital of the Cherokee Nation). Mrs. LoVette was employed as Education Director for the United Methodist Children's Home. After two productive years, Dr. LoVette was given an ultimatum by several School Board members that required the firing of a large number of staff members. The ultimatum came in the form of a list of staff members whom the representative Board Member said were incompetent: "These people are all incompetent and if you can't get rid of them you are incompetent." LoVette refused and began a search for yet another position.

The move to Louisiana to a superintendency in East Feliciana parish was made reluctantly because family and friends would be left far behind. The Louisiana parish posed many challenges since many of the white parents had opted to send their children to private schools in an effort to avoid racial integration. Making improvement in the district would be difficult because of these tensions and also because three central office administrators, who were long-time residents of the district, had been applicants for the position of superintendent. After serving 1 year of a 4-year contract (granted by a 7 to 6 split vote—split on racial lines), LoVette was offered a position in Educational Leadership at Southeastern Louisiana University in Hammond, Louisiana. The change was welcome, but the salary reduction (nearly a 40%) was a shock. After 3 busy years, teaching a variety of courses, writing, presenting, and doing the things necessary for promotion and tenure, he moved north to Northeast Louisiana University (The University of Louisiana at Monroe). The move improved his salary substantially and he was advanced to the rank of associate professor. He was advanced to the rank of professor during his 5th year and subsequently became Endowed Professor. He continues to teach Educational Leadership courses, always emphasizing application and practicality, while performing a variety of other duties with energy and enthusiasm.